STYLES, KEITH
WORKING DRAWINGS HANDBOOK
011044452

72.021 S93

1104452

WITHDRAWN FROM STOCK

WORKING DRAWINGS
HANDBOOK

WORKING DRAWINGS HANDBOOK

Second Edition

Keith Styles

The Architectural Press : London

First published in 1982 by the Architectural Press Limited,
9 Queen Anne's Gate, London SW1H 9BY

Second edition 1986

© Keith Styles 1982, 1986

British Library Cataloguing in Publication Data

Styles, Keith
   Architects' working drawings.
   1. Architectural drawing—Technique
   I. Title
   720'.28'4   N2708

ISBN 0 85139 712 3

All rights reserved. No part of this publication may be reproduced, stored in a retrieval system, or transmitted, in any form or by any means, electronic, mechanical, photocopying, recording or otherwise, without the prior permission of the publishers. Such permission, if granted, is subject to a fee depending on the nature of the use.

Printed and bound in Great Britain
by Mackays of Chatham

Contents

1 The structure of information 1
The problem 1
The structure of working drawings 4

2 Types of drawing 21
The location drawing 21
Component drawings 40
Sub-component drawings 52
The assembly drawing 52
The schedule 59
Pictorial views 64
Specification 64

3 Draughtsmanship 66
Drawing reproduction 66
Materials 66
Techniques 67
Drawing conventions 72
Dimensioning 74
Lettering 79

4 Working drawing management 84
The objective 84
Pre-requisites for Stage F 84
Planning the set 92
The drawing register 95
Other consultants' drawings 102
Drawing office programming 104
Introducing new methods 104

5 Other methods 106
Towards the future 106

Appendix 1 Building elements and external features 118
Appendix 2 Conventions for doors and windows 120
Appendix 3 Symbols indicating materials 122
Appendix 4 Electrical, telecommunications and fire symbols 124
Appendix 5 Non-active lines and symbols 128

Introduction

This book had its origins in the series of articles of the same name published in the *Architects' Journal* in 1976 and 1977. My thanks are due therefore to my fellow contributors to that series, Patricia Tutt, Chris Daltry and David Crawshaw, for many stimulating discussions during its production, and to the *Architects' Journal* for allowing me to reproduce material from it.

The text however has been re-written, and responsibility for the views expressed and recommendations made is mine alone. I had hoped at the outset to illustrate the book with actual drawings taken from live projects, but for various reasons this proved to be impracticable. Invariably the scale was wrong, or the drawing was too big, or would not reproduce satisfactorily, or was too profusely covered with detail irrelevant to the immediate purpose.

In the event the drawings in the book have been drawn for it especially, or have been re-drawn for it from source material supplied by others. My thanks for providing such source material are due to Messrs Oscar Garry and Partners, the Department of Health and Social Security, Messrs Kenchington Little and Partners, The Property Services Agency and my own practice, Peter Leach Associates.

Finally, I must record my enduring gratitude to my wife, Alison Styles, who not only produced a typescript from my illegibly hand written draft but managed to survive my bad temper during the writing of it.

Preface to Second Edition

In producing this second edition I have taken the opportunity of up-dating and expanding certain sections of the book, and of making corrections to others.

There is an obvious difficulty with a book such as this, whose object is to set out what may be considered good practice, that it may deal with its subject in too great a depth for the experienced practitioner, while at the same time assuming too great a prior knowledge on the part of the student reader. Those comments on the book which have been received since its publication suggest that its readership includes a high proportion of the young and inexperienced and, in view of the cursory way in which the whole field of building communications appears to be dealt with in the schools, I have thought it right in the present edition to increase rather than reduce the explanatory detail. In particular the captions have been expanded so that the illustrations make their point better without constant reference to the text.

One point was made in the first edition, but is worth making again here. The illustrations have been selected – indeed, in many instances, devised – solely for their function in illustrating points made in the text, and are not presented as working details to be used for any other purpose.

1 The structure of information

1.1 *Hellman's view of the problem*

The problem

No one who has delivered drawings to site and overheard the foreman's jocular reference to a 'fresh set of comics' having arrived will deny that the quality of architects' working drawings in general is capable of improvement. In some measure we have all of us suffered more or less justifiable accusations of inaccuracy, inadequacy and incomprehensibility; and yet drawings are prepared and issued with the best of intentions. Few offices deliberately skimp the job, despite economic pressures and time constraints, for the consequences of inadequate or incorrect information being passed to the builder loom frighteningly behind every contract. We do our genuine best, and still things go wrong which might have been avoided; still information is found to be missing, or vague, or incorrect (**1.1**).

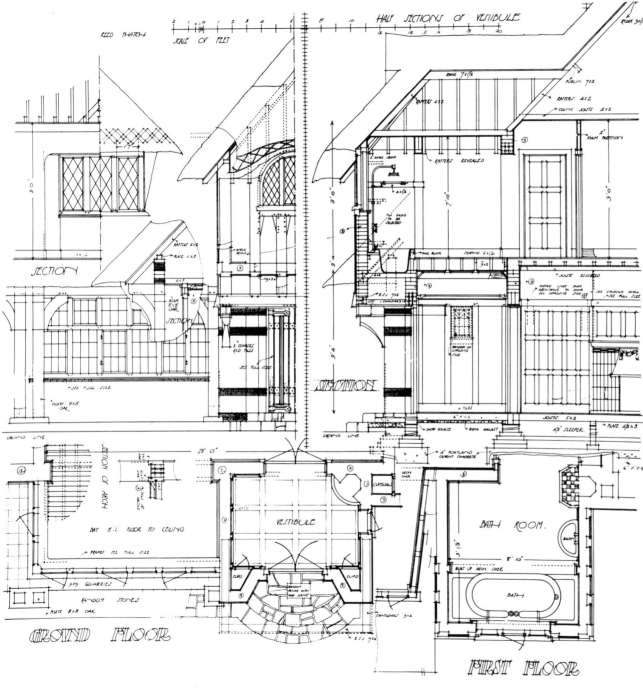

The 1973 UK Building Research Establishment's current paper 'Working drawings in use' lists a depressing number of defects which the authors found giving rise to site queries. Those defects include:
- unco-ordinated drawings (ie information from different sources found to be in conflict)
- errors—items of information incorrect
- failures in transmission (ie information produced and available but not put in the right hands)
- omissions—items of information accidentally missing
- poor presentation (ie the drawing or set of drawings was complete, but confusing to read).

Analysis of this list suggests that the defects spring from different causes—some from an inadequate understanding of the users' needs, some from an indisciplined approach to the problems of presenting a complex package of information, and some from faulty project management procedures. That the problems seem to arise more frequently in relation to architects' drawings than to those of other disciplines merely illustrates how the difficulty is compounded by the complicated nature of the architect's work and the diversity of the information he has to provide. The structural engineer need only adopt a simple cross-referencing system to enable him to link any structural member back to a general arrangement drawing; but for an architect economically to give precise and simply understood directions about, say, a door set—involving a range of variables which include door, frame, architrave, finishes, materials and ironmongery—a communications method of some complexity will be required. Where is such a method to be found? (**1.2**)

Problems of communication
The *Handbook of Architectural Practice and Management* (published by the Royal Institute of British Architects)

1.2 *House at Gerrards Cross by A. Jessop Hardwick, c. 1905. A typical working drawing of its era, in both its draughting techniques and its obsessive use of every inch of the drawing sheet (RIBA Drawings Collection)*

THE STRUCTURE OF INFORMATION

points out, 'As with all technical communication, the user's needs are the prime consideration'. Whoever the user is—and the users of a set of drawings will be many and various—he has the right to expect that the information given to him will be:
- an accurate record of the designer's intentions
- clearly expressed and easily understood
- comprehensive and sufficiently detailed for its purpose
- easily retrievable from the mass of other information with which, inevitably, it will be combined.

It is the purpose of this book to consider these four requirements in detail and hopefully to propose techniques for satisfying them.

There is a fifth and fundamental requirement, of course. The information conveyed must be technically sound, and if this is not the case then all the careful draughting and cross-referencing will not be sufficient to prevent disaster. This aspect, however, lies outside the scope of the present book which must concern itself only with the adequate documentation of technical decisions already made at an earlier stage. In RIBA Plan of Work terminology, the decisions belong to stage E; their documentation belongs to stage F.

The plan of work

Since what we shall be looking at is in effect a series of disciplines, and since the plan of work is the overriding discipline into which the working drawing process is integrated, it is probably worthwhile reminding ourselves of the plan of work at the outset. Table I shows it in its entirety, with descriptions of its elements simplified somewhat from the original in the interests of brevity.

Frequent reference to the plan of work will be made in this book, for it is important that stage F production drawings should be seen in the context of the whole architectural process, forming the vital link between the designer's intention and the builder's execution of it. The successful implementation of many of the techniques to be dealt with here will depend upon proper procedures having been carried out at earlier stages, whilst the whole *raison d'être* of the drawing set lies in the stages following its production.

The users

There are many users of a set of drawings and each may put it to more than one use. Unless the set is to be redrawn expensively to suit the ideal requirements of each, then priorities must be established and compromises accepted. Consider the following functions of a set of drawings (the list is by no means exhaustive). It forms for different people and at different times:
- a basis for tendering ('bidding', in USA)
- a contractual commitment
- a source for the preparation of other documents
- a statement of intent for the purpose of obtaining statutory consents
- a framework for establishing nominated sub-contractors or suppliers
- a source for the preparation of shop drawings
- a shopping list for the ordering of materials
- a construction manual
- a model for developing the construction programme
- a supervising document
- a record of variations from the contract
- a base document for measurement of the completed works and preparation of the final accounts
- a base document for defects liability inspection
- a record of the completed structure
- a source of feedback.

It will be noted that the majority of these uses involve the contractor and clearly his needs are paramount, if only for the purely legal reason that it is he who will be contractually committed to the employer to build what the architect tells him to. They may be separated into three main activities, and any drawing method must satisfy all three if it is to prove viable.

Activity 1 The procurement of all the necessary materials and components. For this he will need the following information in a form in which it can be identified readily and extracted for ordering purposes:

> A specification of the material to be used, which can be referred back simply to the drawings and the bills of quantities.
> Drawings and schedules of all components which he is to provide (doors, windows, etc), and which constitute measured items in the bills of quantities.
> Drawings and schedules from which outside manufacturers' products may be ordered, and which provide design criteria against which manufacturers' shop drawings may be checked.

Activity 2 The deployment of plant and labour. For this he will need:

> Drawings showing the extent of each trade's involvement.
> A 'construction manual' describing, by means of annotated drawings, the way in which each trade is to operate and which is explicit enough to ensure that no local querying or decision-making will be necessary.
> An objective and realistic description of the quality standards required and the methods to be employed.

Activity 3 The preparation of a programme and decision on a method of operation. For this he needs:

> Drawings giving an overall picture of his commitment.
> Comprehensive information about the constraints of site, access and programme.
> A summary of his contractual obligations.

The need for a unified system

What we are looking for is a complete information system which will satisfy these different user requirements and which will be at the same time:

- reasonably simple and economical to produce
- simple to understand and to use at all levels
- flexible enough to embrace information produced by various offices—structural, M & E etc
- capable of application to both small and large projects
- appropriate for use in both small and large producing offices.

The importance of the two latter points tends to be underestimated. Given a standard method of procedure a common experience is gradually built up, not only among contractors, but among assistants moving from one project to another within the office, or indeed moving between different offices. Nothing is more disruptive for architect, estimator and contract manager alike than to have to switch constantly from one working method to another.

The Co-ordinating Committee for Project Information is currently engaged in formulating its proposals for a code of practice for building drawings, but until such a code is produced there exists little in the way of definitive guidance as to what a drawing set should consist of, or how it should be organised. Neither does there exist (surprisingly, perhaps) any legal definition of the amount or quality of drawn information which it might be reasonable to expect on a given project.

Given the inherent structure of building information as analysed in the following pages, it is unlikely that a code of practice will eventually emerge differing significantly from the principles outlined here.

One broad limitation must, however, be made at the outset, which will clear a lot of ground and reduce the scope of the present book to more manageable proportions. Despite ingenious alternative methods which have been devised for particular situations, the tripartite concept of drawings, specifications and bills of quantities together forming the complete information package is long enshrined in building contract procedure, and it is not the intention of this book to attempt to disturb that long-standing relationship.

Consideration will be given in a later chapter to what information sometimes given on drawings may be more appropriate to the specification; but other than that this book will concern itself solely with drawings, regarding these as the base documents in the information package which it is the role of the specification to amplify, the bills to quantify (**1.3**).

Table 1 The RIBA outline plan of work

Stage	Purpose of work and Decisions to be reached	Tasks to be done	People directly involved	Usual Terminology
A. Inception	To prepare general outline of requirements and plan future action.	Set up client organisation for briefing. Consider requirements, appoint architect.	All client interests, architect.	**Briefing**
B. Feasibility	To provide the client with an appraisal and recommendation in order that he may determine the form in which the project is to proceed, ensuring that it is feasible, functionally, technically and financially.	Carry out studies of user requirements, site conditions, planning, design, and cost etc., as necessary to reach decisions.	Clients' representatives, architects, engineers and QS according to nature of project.	
C. Outline Proposals	To determine general approach to layout, design and construction in order to obtain authoritative approval of the client on the outline proposals and accompanying report.	Develop the brief further. Carry out studies on user requirements, technical problems, planning, design and costs, as necessary to reach decisions.	All client interest, architects engineers, QS and specialists as required.	**Sketch Plans**
D. Scheme Design	To complete the brief and decide on particular proposals, including planning arrangement appearance, constructional method, outline specification, and cost, and to obtain all approvals.	Final development of the brief, full design of the project by architect, preliminary design by engineers, preparation of cost plan and full explanatory report. Submission of proposals for all approvals.	All client interests, architects, engineers, QS and specialists and all statutory and other approving authorities.	
Brief should not be modified after this point				
E. Detail Design	To obtain final decision on every matter related to design, specification, construction and cost.	Full design of every part and component of the building by collaboration of all concerned. Complete cost checking of designs.	Architects, QS, engineers and specialists, contractor (if appointed).	**Working Drawings**

The structure of working drawings

Every set of working drawings consisting of more than one sheet is structured, for it represents a more or less conscious decision on the part of the draughtsman to put certain information on one sheet of paper, and certain other information on others. Even were the reason for doing so simply that there is insufficient space on a single sheet of paper, a selection has still to be made of what to put on each sheet, and a sensible

Table I The RIBA outline plan of work (continued)

Stage	Purpose of work and Decisions to be reached	Tasks to be done	People directly involved	Usual Terminology
Any further change in location, size, shape, or cost after this time will result in abortive work				
F. Production Information	To prepare production information and make final detailed decisions to carry out work.	Preparation of final production information i.e. drawings, schedules and specifications.	Architects, engineers and specialists, contractor (if appointed).	
G. Bills of Quantities	To prepare and complete all information and arrangements for obtaining tender.	Preparation of Bills of Quantities and tender documents.	Architects, QS, contractor (if appointed).	
H. Tender Action	Action as recommended in paras. 7–14 inclusive of 'Selective Tendering'*	Action as recommended in paras. 7–14 inclusive of 'Selective Tendering'*	Architects, QS, engineers, contractor, client.	
J. Project Planning	Action in accordance with paras. 5–10 inclusive of 'Project Management'*	Action in accordance with paras. 5–10 inclusive of 'Project Management'*	Contractor, sub-contractors.	Site Operations
K. Operations on site	Action in accordance with paras. 11–14 inclusive of 'Project Management'*	Action in accordance with paras. 11–14 inclusive of 'Project Management'*	Architects, engineers, contractors, sub-contractors, QS, client.	
L. Completion	Action in accordance with paras. 15–18 inclusive of 'Project Management'*	Action in accordance with paras. 15–18 inclusive of 'Project Management'*	Architects, engineers, contractor, QS, client.	
M. Feed-Back	To analyse the management, construction and performance of the project.	Analysis of job records. Inspections of completed building. Studies of building in use.	Architects, engineers, QS, contractor, client.	

* *Publication of National Joint Consultative Council of Architects, Quantity Surveyors and Builders.*

basis for that division has to be determined.

Indeed, the simplest of single sheet applications to a local authority for approval under the Building Regulations for the erection of a garage is likely to contain a small scale plan showing the site in relation to the surrounding neighbourhood as well as a dimensioned plan of the building itself. This in effect acknowledges the existence of some informational hierarchy within which certain different aspects of instruction about the building may sensibly be given in different places and in different ways (**1.4**).

In the following pages we shall be not so much seeking to impose a method of doing this as seeking out the structure inherent in the whole concept of building information, and trying to reflect it in the form that the information package will take.

THE STRUCTURE OF INFORMATION

Let us start our search at the point where the ultimate end product of the entire communications exercise is to be found—the building site.

What, where and how?
The information that an operative needs to know about each element of the building he is called upon to construct may be classified into three distinct types:
1. He needs to know *what* it is that he has to install or erect. Whether it be window frame, brick or cubic metre of concrete, he needs to know certain information about its nature and physical dimensions.
2. He needs to know *where* it is to be placed. This demands pictorial and dimensional information regarding its relationship to the building as a whole.
3. He needs to know *how* it is to be placed or fixed in relation to its immediately neighbouring elements.

Clearly these three questions—*what*, *where* and *how*—are fundamental to the business of building communications, and demand a variety of replies in practice if they are to be answered satisfactorily and without ambiguity. It may be useful to reflect for a moment on the degree of depth and comprehensiveness that may be required of these answers.

If the designer has devised a precise solution to the building problem set him by his client, then the information to be conveyed to the builder must be of sufficient detail to enable the unique nature of that solution to be appreciated and converted into physical building terms by a variety of people, most of whom will be unfamiliar with the original problem, and unaware of the chain of thought processes which has given rise to its solution.

So if we are dealing with a window the single question—What window?—may proliferate into a large and varied series: what are its overall dimensions; what does it look like; what material is it made from; what is its glass thickness; what furniture does it have; what are its finishes? These and many other questions will arise from consideration of the nature of a single component.

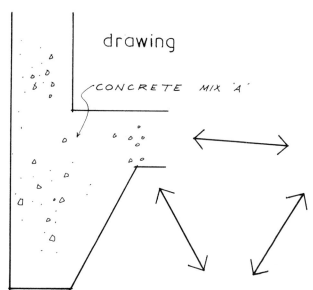

1.3 *Drawings, specification and bills of quantities. Each has a clearly defined role in the information package*

Similarly we need to know where in the building it is to be installed, implying the need for dimensional information in three planes; and how it is to be installed—how it sits in relation to the lintol above it, how it relates to the vertical DPCs in the adjacent wall cavities, how many fixing points are required and what is the nature of their fixing. And so on.

The amount of information required so that the description of any aspect of the building will be unambiguous must always be a matter for intelligent consideration. The strength and density of bricks forming footings below ground level, for instance, will be fit subjects for precise description, whereas their colour will not.

But two fundamental principles emerge which will be found to hold good at all times.
1. All building information may be classified into three basic categories, depending upon which of the three basic questions—how, where and what—it purports to answer.
2. All building information is hierarchic in its nature and proceeds from the general to the particular.

This latter observation requires some discussion, because the sequence in which the three questions emerge which were posed at the start of this section may suggest that the seeker after information starts with the component and its nature, and then works outwards to a consideration of where and how to install it. This sequence is in fact occasionally true—the window manufacturer, for example, would tend to consider the type of windows he was being called upon to make before determining how many of them there were in the building, and how they were distributed throughout it.

But in general terms the reverse is true. Almost every user of the information package will wish to know that there is a wall of finite dimensions with windows in it which forms the outer boundary of the building, before seeking to determine the various forms that the windows might take or the precise nature of the bricks and their pointing.

Since this is also the manner in which the designer will logically work, there is little difficulty, and every advantage, in devising a system in which the search for information starts with the question Where?, and in which the answer to this question provides within itself the indication as to where the answers may be found to the supplementary questions What? and How?

Primary structuring—by information type
What has been outlined is a method of primary

THE STRUCTURE OF INFORMATION

structuring of information according to its type and which may be summarised and named as follows:

- *Location* information, answering the questions: *where* are components to be built or installed, and *where* may further information about them be found?
- *Component* information, answering the question: *what* is the component like?
- *Assembly* information, answering the question: *how* are the various components to be related one to another—how are they to be assembled?

This type of structure, and the search pattern it generates, is illustrated in **1.5**.

The schedule: Into this neatly classified system must now be introduced that somewhat hybrid creature, the schedule. And here again some fundamental questioning is needed to ensure that it will fulfil its proper function.

The idea of using written schedules, or lists of information, instead of drawings exists in most information systems and has its source in a variety of motives, not all of them necessarily valid. It is assumed that they are economical of drawing office time; that quantity surveyors, contractors and suppliers alike all welcome them; that they provide a ready check that the information conveyed is comprehensive.

These reasons do not always stand up to close examination. Schedules are only economical if they are simpler than the drawings they replace; the architect should not necessarily be doing other people's jobs for them; suppliers more often than not produce their own schedules because the architect's schedule is not in a form which they find usable, and some schedules attempt to provide so much information in so complicated a form that mistakes and omissions readily occur.

Nevertheless, they have a role to play, and used sensibly and with forethought they form an essential element in the information package.

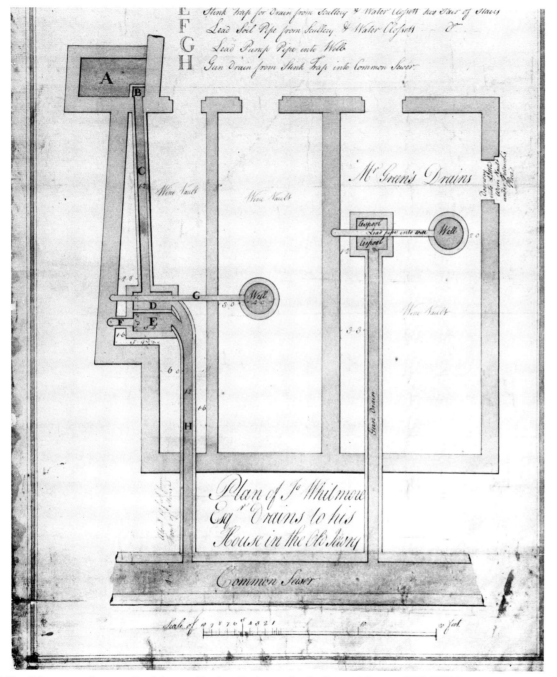

1.4 *Detail from an early example of elementalisation. Drainage plan by James Adam, c. 1775 (RIBA Drawings Collection)*

WORKING DRAWINGS HANDBOOK

Some principles affecting scheduling may be enumerated:

> Their initial function is to identify and list components possessing common characteristics—eg windows, doors, manhole covers, etc.
>
> They should not attempt to provide comprehensive information about the component; they should serve rather as an index to where the relevant information may be found.
>
> They should initiate a simple search pattern for the retrieval of component, sub-component and assembly information.
>
> They are only worth providing if the component in question has more than one variable. For instance, if you have windows of three different sizes which are identical in every other respect, then size is the only variable and you may as well write 'Window Type 1' on the Location Plan as 'Window No 1'. But if each window size may be fixed either into a brick wall or a pre-cast concrete panel then the assembly information required is a second variable.
>
> Window Type 1 may be combined with jamb detail type 1 or type 2, and it is for this greater degree of complexity that it is preferable to prepare a schedule.

The great virtue of the schedule is that it can direct you to a vast amount of information about a given component in a way that would be impossible to achieve by any system of direct referencing from a location drawing. Consider a window—thirty-seventh, shall we say, of fifty on the second floor of a multi-storey block of offices. The method chosen for giving it a unique reference is unimportant for the moment—W2/37 is as good a piece of shorthand as any for the purpose—but it is obvious that this simple means of identification may be shown equally on a drawing or a schedule (**1.6**).

Thus, there are two ways of providing a catalogue of the windows on the job, in which W2/37 is seen to take its place between W2/36 and W2/38. But if we were now to add to the drawing a fuller description of what W2/37 in fact consists of, then we should meet an immediate difficulty—there just is not space to do it (**1.7**).

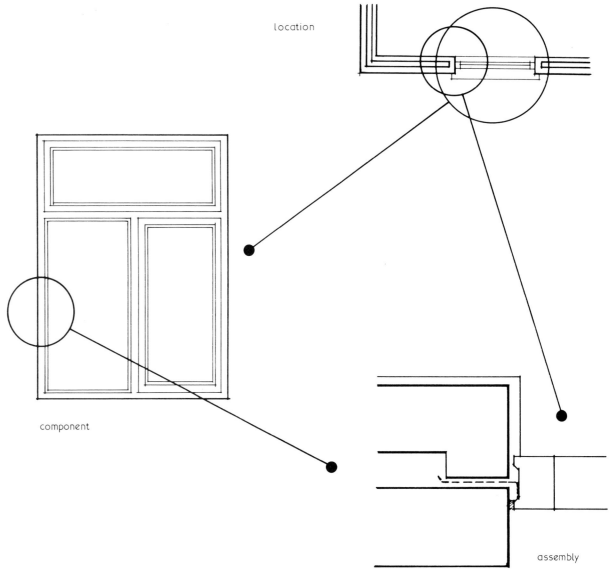

1.5 *The fundamental search pattern generated by the questions Where?, What? and How?*

Consequently when it is considered that the information given only scratches the surface of what the recipient really needs to know, and that similar information will need to be provided about W2/1 to W2/50—to name but the windows on the second floor—it becomes

THE STRUCTURE OF INFORMATION

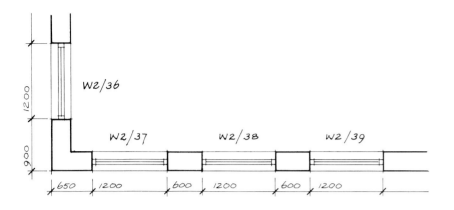

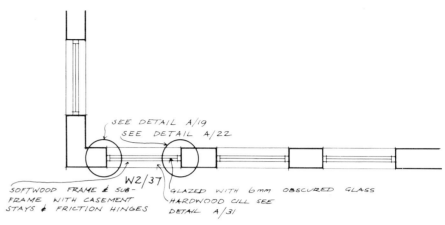

1.7 *The location plan is an inappropriate medium for recording the diverse characteristics of each component. Detail of this order can only be given elsewhere – in a specification or in other drawings to which the schedules point the way*

type / no.	size	etc.
W2/36	1200	
W2/37	1200	
W2/38	1200	
W2/39	1200	

1.6 *Simple identification of components may be recorded on either a schedule or a location plan*

window no.	window type	width	height	component detail no.	l.h. jamb detail no.	r.h. jamb detail no.	cill detail no.	head detail no.	etc.
W2/36	WA	1200	1800	C/15	A/19	A/22	A/31	A/36	
W2/37	WB	1200	2100	C/19	A/19	A/22	A/31	A/42	
W2/38	WA	1200	1800	C/15	A/19	A/22	A/31	A/36	
W2/39	WC	1200	2400	C/20	A/17	A/18	A/30	A/37	

1.8 *The schedule provides a simple and economical index to a variety of information*

apparent that not only will there be insufficient room on the drawing to make this method feasible, there will be insufficient drawing office time and money available to make it an economic starter. The schedule does it so much better (**1.8**).

Given the presence of schedules in the package, the search pattern given in **1.6** becomes simpler and more directly focussed. The location drawing is still the starting point, but now the searcher is directed from it to the schedule, and from there to the various sources of assembly and component information (**1.9**).

Further consideration will be given later to the most suitable format for schedules and to the areas of information which lend themselves most readily to scheduling. All that remains to be settled for the moment is what sort of an animal this hybrid most resembles. Is it a drawing, or some other form of document? If a drawing, then what type of drawing is it?

In practice it does not really matter provided that all the implications of the choice have been fully considered, and that having made your decision you are consistent in sticking to it.

The schedule's function is primarily that of an index, and as such it will at different times direct the searcher towards assembly drawing, component drawing, specification, trade literature and, possibly, the bills of quantities. If considered as a drawing then it clearly possesses all the directive qualities of a location drawing, and could be so regarded. But it will inevitably be of a different nature—and indeed size—from the other location drawings in the package, and its status as such puts it in an anomalous situation when used in conjunction with other documents—as an adjunct to the bills of quantities, for example.

Maximum flexibility in use is therefore achieved by acknowledging the hybrid nature of the schedule for what it is, and by treating it as an independent form of document in its own right, capable equally of being bound into a set of drawings or into a specification.

The package is nearly complete. It requires two further categories of drawing to render it entirely comprehensive, however. They may be dealt with quite quickly.

Sub-component drawings: First, it will become desirable at times to illustrate how a component itself is made. The frame sections of a timber window, for example, are often better shown separately from the drawing showing the window itself, for they may well be applicable to a number of windows whose overall sizes and appearances are widely different. Yet to term the drawing showing these sections a component drawing is inaccurate, as well as being potentially confusing. In the hierarchy of information it is clearly one step lower and more detailed.

It is, in fact, a sub-component drawing and there is a place for it as such in the set (**1.10**).

Information drawings: Secondly, there is a class of drawing which conveys information, not so much about the building and its elements as about the building's background. Such matters as the site survey, records of adjoining buildings, light envelope diagrams, bore hole analyses all fall into this category. They have this feature in common, which distinguishes them from the

1.9 *The fundamental search pattern of* **1.5** *now runs through the schedule*

1.10 *The sub-component drawing illustrates how the component itself is made*

THE STRUCTURE OF INFORMATION

SUMMARY OF BORE HOLE LOGS.

PENETRATION TESTS SHOWN THUS S(18) STANDARD PENETRATION TESTS (BLOWS/FT)
C(11) CONE PENETRATION TESTS (BLOWS/FT)

1.11 Typical information drawing – this record of bore hole findings provides the contractor with useful background information but gives no instruction about the building

other drawings in the package, that they convey information without giving instructions (**1.11**).

The complete primary structure: The complete primary structure is summarised in **1.12**. It is worth noting that this complete drawing package, which has to be all things to all men, is now capable of sub-division into smaller packages, each of which is tailored to suit the needs of the individual recipient. The site foreman needs to know the position and size of the window he has to install, but has no interest in the manner in which it is made in the joiner's shop. Similarly, the local authority will not require the complete set of drawings for approval (even though the extravagant demands of certain Building Control officers in this respect may induce in frustrated practitioners a somewhat cynical smile at this statement).

With occasional exceptions, however, the drawing set may be used as shown here, with attendant advantages of order and economy. The focal position of the schedule is well demonstrated.

Secondary structuring
The good old-fashioned working drawing floor plan—ancestor of the location plan and aimed at embracing every piece of information necessary for the erection of the building—still survives in places, but its defects are now so generally recognised that it is possibly unnecessary to spend much time in demonstrating them. Figure **1.13**, taken almost at random from such a drawing, shows the disadvantages.

The sheet is cluttered with information, making it extremely difficult to read. The notes and references fill every available corner, and in an attempt to crowd too much information into too small a compass, the draughtsman has had to resort to a lettering style of microscopic dimensions. Any alteration to it would be difficult both to achieve and to identify. (Figure **1.2** also illustrates the defects inherent in the 'one drawing' approach.)

This is a case of one drawing attempting to do the work of several, and simplicity, legibility and common sense would all be better served if there were several drawings to replace it. Let us consider the various ways in which the crowded information might be distributed.

The Department of the Environment report, 'Structuring Project Information', published in 1972 listed no fewer than nine separate non-traditional systems then identifiable which included in their make-up some degree of information structuring. The sixties, of course, had been a time of widespread and largely unco-ordinated experimentation in building communications techniques, generated by an increasing demand on the resources of an over-stretched profession and building industry, and a growing awareness of the inefficiency and waste of time on building sites being caused by inadequate documentation. Not all the systems were at that time sufficiently well tested to allow a genuine evaluation of their merits.

Now, nearly a decade later, we are in a better position to obtain a proper perspective view of the field, and the problem becomes somewhat clearer. Some of the communications systems then presenting themselves for consideration are now seen to be so closely associated with the requirements of specific organisations or constructional systems that they lack universal applicability. Others, reliant upon a more radical re-fashioning of the bills of quantities than is envisaged

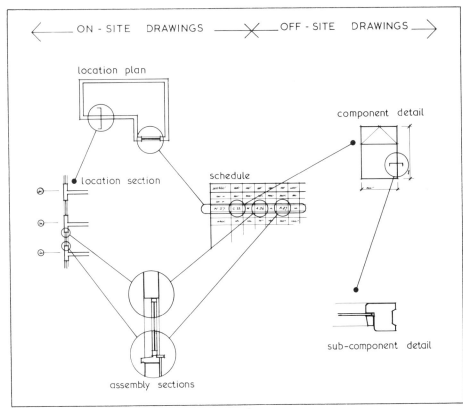

1.12 *The complete primary structure of building drawings information*

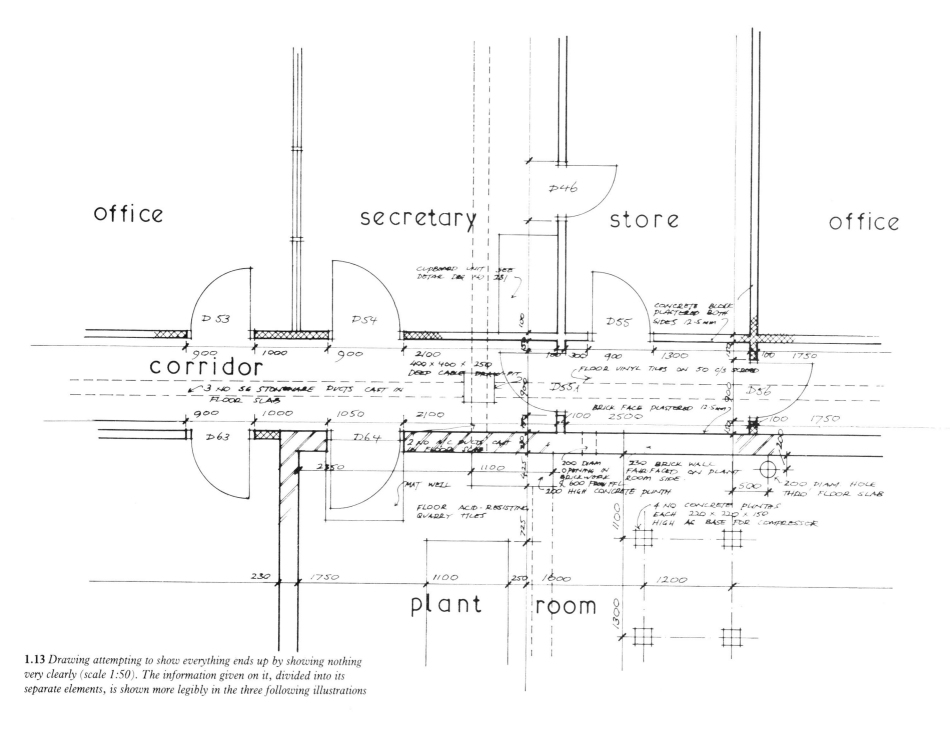

1.13 *Drawing attempting to show everything ends up by showing nothing very clearly (scale 1:50). The information given on it, divided into its separate elements, is shown more legibly in the three following illustrations*

WORKING DRAWINGS HANDBOOK

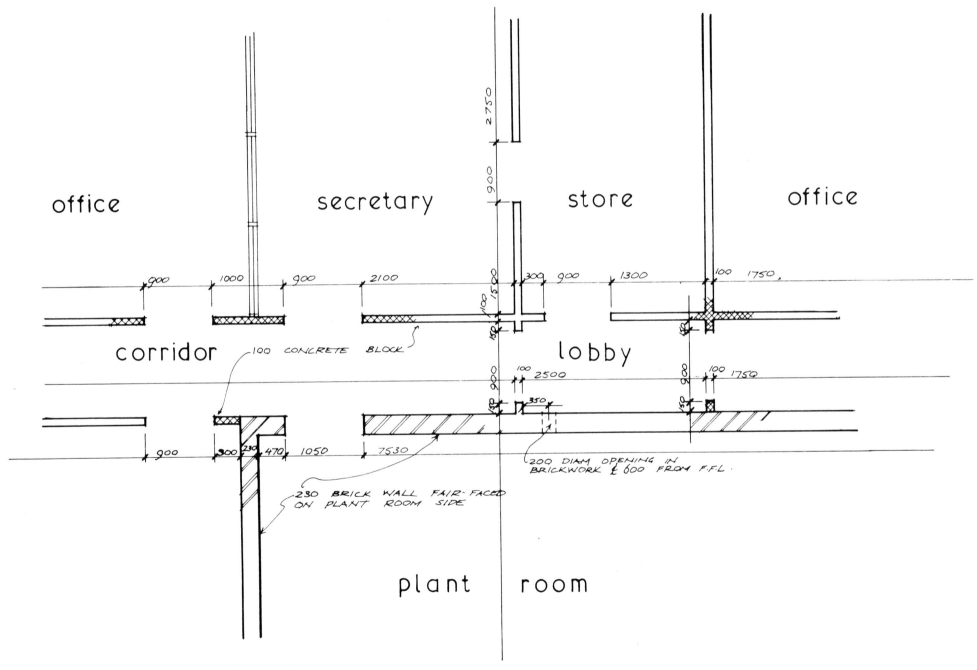

1.14 *Elemental version of* 1.13 *dealing with walls (scale 1:50)*

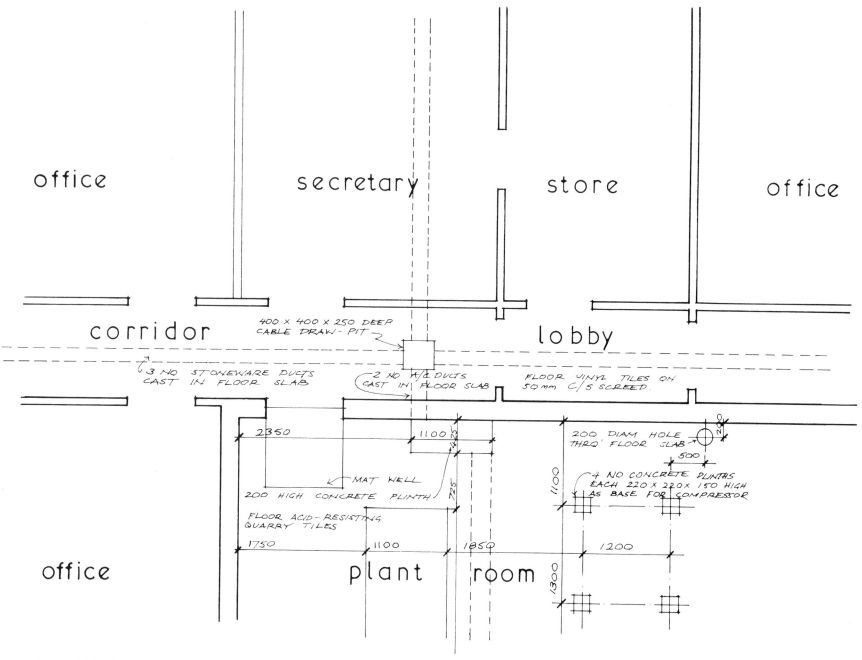

1.15 *Elemental version of* **1.13** *dealing with the floor (scale 1:50)*

WORKING DRAWINGS HANDBOOK

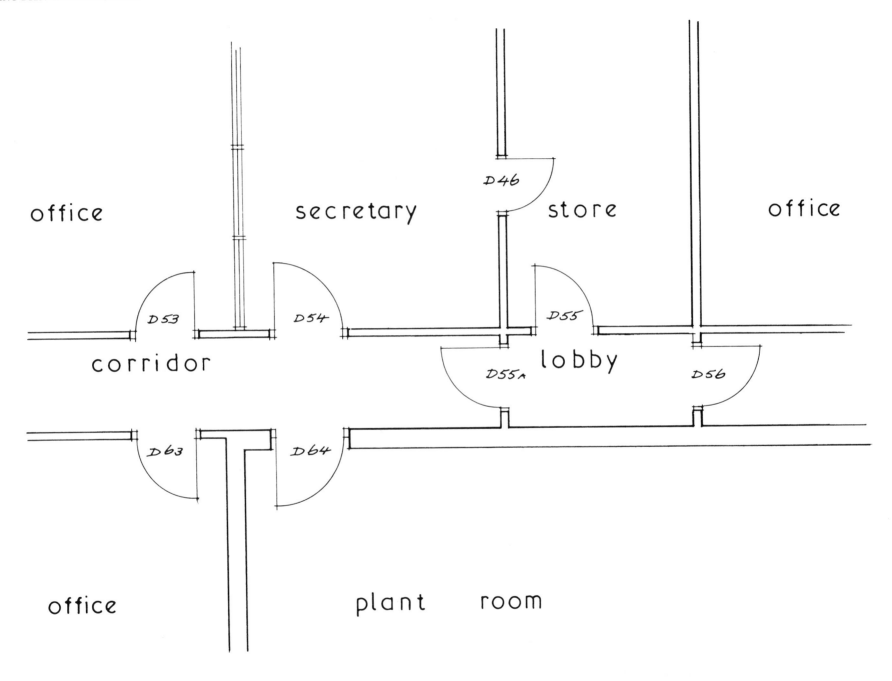

1.16 *Elemental version of* **1.13** *dealing with doors (scale 1:50)*

here, offer pointers to the future and are discussed in chapter 5.

All accept the primary structuring of drawn information represented in this book by the location/component/assembly format. Where they tend to diverge is in their approach to secondary structuring, and their methods of identifying and coding it.

The building operation, and indeed the completed building, may be considered in a number of ways. You may regard it, for example, as an assemblage of different materials. To some extent the specification does just that, describing with precision the type of sand, the type of cement and the size of aggregate to be used, as well as describing their admixture into concrete (the point at which the bills of quantities take an interest).

You may look at it, on the other hand, as a series of different trade activities, in which case you would tend to regard as one package of information all work done by the carpenter, and as another package all work done by the plumber. Again, traditional bills of quantities are structured on these lines, and the concept lies at the heart of the standard method of measurement.

In drawing terms, however, neither sub-division relates very happily to the architectural realities. To the quantity surveyor one cubic metre of concrete may be very like another, but when one forms part of the foundations and another part of the roof slab it is over-simplistic to suggest that both should form part of a series of 'concrete' or 'concretor' drawings.

Drawings are by definition concerned with the perceived form of the building, and if we are to sub-divide them then a breakdown into the different elements of their form is more logical than an attempt to classify them by either material or trade subdivisions.

So let us return to the cluttered example shown in **1.13** and separate it into three elements chosen at random, collecting information about the walls on to one drawing, the floor on another and the doors on a third (**1.14, 1.15** and **1.16**).

At once we can see what we are doing. The notes and references to other drawings are relatively few and sparsely distributed, so that they catch the eye, and plenty of space is left for further annotation should this become desirable during the course of the project. Furthermore, to anyone who knows how this particular set of drawings is sub-divided the search pattern for any aspect of the building is straightforward. If he wants to know about windows he can go straight to the location drawing dealing with windows, from which point the search pattern described previously can proceed within the narrow confines of window information. The general search pattern, shown diagrammatically in **1.17** now follows a series of paths, each related to a specific aspect of the building (**1.18**).

The advantages of this are two-fold. In the first place the designer now has a framework upon which to display his information and in the second place the user has an authoritative guide through the informational labyrinth.

Structuring by building element: Within the framework of a primary structuring by information type, the information to be conveyed is sub-divided by building element and this constitutes the secondary structuring of the drawing set.

To establish the possible means of achieving this we should start by looking at the various ways in which the building fabric may be regarded. Consider the diagram in **1.19**.

It is difficult to visualise any space-enclosing structure, no matter how primitive, which did not possess elements falling within one or other of these four categories. A little thought, however, will suggest that this is an over-simplification, and that a minimal sub-division of elements would look much more like **1.20**.

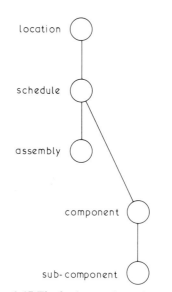
1.17 *The fundamental search pattern*

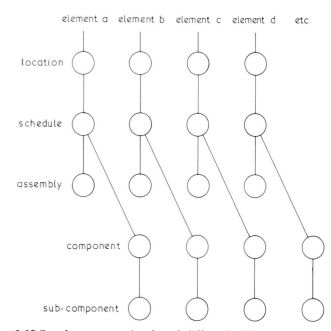
1.18 *Search pattern running through different building elements*

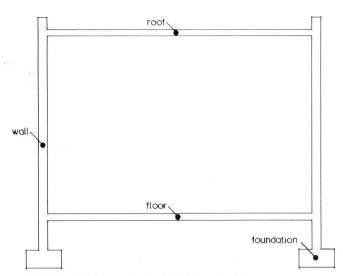

1.19 *The simplest possible sub-division of building structure*

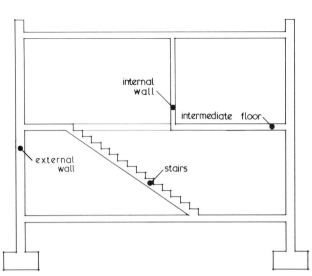

1.20 *Sub-division of building structure into structural elements*

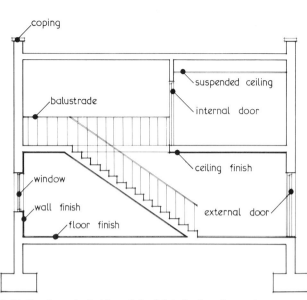

1.21 *Further sub-division of the fabric leads to increasing complexity*

The elements here have one common feature—they are all structural. We may introduce other elements, but it is apparent that we are then setting up another hierarchy of information analogous to the hierarchy established when considering types of information (**1.21**).

It is one thing to recognise the existence of this hierarchy, and another thing altogether to set it down in simple and universally acceptable terms. The trouble with hierarchic systems—in building communications as in politics—is that they tend to be complex, difficult to understand and self-defeating when applied too rigidly. Their great advantage—in building communications at any rate—is that they offer the user access at the level most appropriate to his purpose. So we are looking for a method of elementalising the building which fulfils the following requirements:

- It should be simple to understand
- It should be universally applicable
- It should operate on a number of levels, permitting a greater or lesser sub-division of information depending upon the size and complexity of the building in question.

Home-made systems: It is not difficult to devise your own systems to meet these requirements. Indeed, in practice many offices do, varying the method each time to suit the complexity of the job in hand. Within the overall primary location/component/assembly framework, for instance, to divide the drawings on a small project into, say, brickwork (series B), windows (series W), doors (series D) etc might be one such method. The precise method of sub-division and of coding is less important than recognising the existence of an inherent primary and secondary structure.

CI/SfB

A fully developed method is readily available, however, which fulfils most of the requirements of an elemental secondary structuring system, and which has the advantage of being already well-established for other purposes. This is the CI/SfB method of information classification and, while it has its detractors, who legitimately point to certain weaknesses in detail, it has so many advantages that on balance it must be recommended. Certainly it forms the basis of most of the drawings illustrated in subsequent chapters. Its virtues are:

> It is the most widely known and used classification method available to the building industry.
> It is comprehensive in its scope, offering opportunities for uniting the drawings (with their emphasis on building elements) and the specification and bills of quantities (with their emphasis on materials) into a common terminology.
> It is capable of operation at all levels of sophistication, making it suitable for both large and small projects.
> It is compatible with use of the National Building Specification.
> It is compatible, or would appear to be so, with developments in the field of computer graphics.

The complete CI/SfB system is undoubtedly complex and many people shy away from it, frightened at the prospect of having such a sophisticated sledge-hammer to crack such small nuts as are the mainstay of the average practice. This is a pity, for that aspect of CI/SfB which is of greatest relevance to the drawing office is in fact of a disarming simplicity. (It is certainly less complicated than some home-made systems that one has encountered over the years.)

Before looking at this aspect in detail, however, let us look briefly at the whole range of the CI/SfB system of classification.

There are five tables in the complete CI/SfB matrix (see box below).

All of these tables are used for library classification; and indeed it is possible to use them in addition as a framework for complete project documentation, upon which every site, drawing office and administrative activity may be fitted. But this is better left to the doctrinaire, the highly ambitious, or the managers of extremely large and complex projects, where the organisational requirements are so great that they may well benefit from such an approach.

In general terms of drawing classification, we may safely discard tables 0 and 4 as being irrelevant to our purpose, set aside tables 2 and 3 for later, when the question of correlation between drawings and specification is being considered, and concentrate our attentions on table 1, which is given in its entirety as Table II (p 20).

CI/SfB table 1: Its hierarchic structure is immediately apparent. Within it each building element may be considered at any of three levels, the level selected being determined by the complexity of the project in question and the need to break down the conveyed information into categories of manageable size. Any element within the building—a lavatory basin, for example—may clearly be regarded as forming part of 'The project in general (– –)'. But it may also be considered as coming within the category of 'Fittings (7–)' (the seventh of the nine vertical columns into which the table is divided). Or, finally, it may be regarded as coming within the quite specific grouping of 'Sanitary, hygiene fittings (74)', the fourth horizontal sub-division of column (7–).

Windows, in similar fashion, may be seen as coming within the (– –), (3–) or (31) headings, terrazzo tiles as (– –), (4–) or (43). And so on.

The primary and secondary information structure is therefore complete, and we are ready to move on to detailed consideration of what each drawing should contain and what it should attempt to convey to the recipient. Before doing so, and since the seventy-five possible facets of table 1 can be a pretty daunting prospect, it may be encouraging if the following points are made:

1. The only possible justification for structuring a set of drawings is that it makes life easier for everybody to do so. The moment this ceases to be the case, the system becomes self-defeating and you would be better off without it.
2. When we talk of elementalising the drawings we are in effect talking exclusively of the location drawings. These are the only drawings which will be drawn elementally in the sense that the same floor plan, for example, may be shown several times to illustrate the various elements contained within it. All other categories of drawing—assembly, component, subcomponent, schedule—will fall within one or other of the elemental sub-divisions: but they will be drawn once only and will appear once only in the drawing set.
3. Although all the facets of table 1 are available, like so many pigeon-holes, to receive the various drawings prepared, there is no particular virtue in trying to use them all. In practice a very few will suffice, even for the largest projects. Never forget the two-fold objective of this secondary structuring, which is to provide both a disciplined framework for the draughtsman and a simple retrieval method for the seeker after information. A drawing set containing a couple of drawings in each of some thirty elemental sub-divisions assists the achievement of neither.
4. Given a true understanding of the objectives, common sense is the paramount consideration.

CI/SfB—The Complete Matrix

Table 0 dealing with physical environment. Such subjects as housing, hospitals and other building types etc come under this heading, and the code is always of the nature B1.

Table 1 dealing with elements—stairs, roofs, ceiling finishes etc. The codes are always bracketed, in the form (24), (27), (45) etc.

Table 2 dealing with the constructed form of products, ie manufactured components. Typical examples would be blockwork—blocks (code F), tubes and pipes (code I) or thin coatings (code V). The codes are always a single upper case letter.

Table 3 dealing with materials—ie the basic materials from which the manufactured components of table 2 are made. Examples would be:

    clay (dried, fired)   (code g2)
    gypsum   (code r2)
    flame-retardant materials (code u4)

The codes consist of a single lower case letter, usually with a single digit as sub-divider, and it will be seen that, when used in conjunction with the codes of table 2, they provide a method of shorthand for quite specific descriptions of components:

    blocks in lightweight aggregate   Fp3
    clay tiles   Ng2
    plywood   Ri4

Table 4 dealing with activities and requirements. In other words, the various techniques involved in the physical process of building, such as:

    testing and evaluation
    demolition.

The codes for these would be, respectively, (Aq) and (D2)

Table II CI/SfB Table 1

(––) Project in general

(1–) Substructure, ground	(2–) Primary elements	(3–) Secondary elements	(4–) Finishes	(5–) Services piped, ducted	(6–) Services, electrical	(7–) Fittings	(8–) Loose furniture equipment	(9–) External, other elements
(10)	(20)	(30)	(40)	(50)	(60)	(70)	(80)	(90) External works
(11) Ground	(21) Walls, external walls	(31) Secondary elements to external walls	(41) Wall finishes, external	(51)	(61) Electrical	(71) Circulation fittings	(81) Circulation, loose equipment	(91)
(12)	(22) Internal walls, partitions	(32) Secondary elements to internal walls	(42) Wall finishes, internal	(52) Waste disposal, drainage	(62) Power	(72) Rest, work fittings	(82) Rest, work loose equipment	(92)
(13) Floor beds	(23) Floors, galleries	(33) Secondary elements to floors	(43) Floor finishes	(53) Liquids supply	(63) Lighting	(73) Culinary fittings	(83) Culinary loose equipment	(93)
(14)	(24) Stairs, ramps	(34) Secondary elements to stairs	(44) Stair finishes	(54) Gases supply	(64) Communications	(74) Sanitary, hygiene fittings	(84) Sanitary, hygiene loose equipment	(94)
(15)	(25)	(35) Suspended ceilings	(45) Ceiling finishes	(55) Space cooling	(65)	(75) Cleaning, maintenance fittings	(85) Cleaning, maintenance loose equipment	(95)
(16) Retaining walls, foundations	(26)	(36)	(46)	(56) Space heating	(66) Transport	(76) Storage, screening fittings	(86) Storage, screening loose equipment	(96)
(17) Pile foundations	(27) Roofs	(37) Secondary elements to roofs	(47) Roof finishes	(57) Air-conditioning, ventilation	(67)	(77) Special activity fittings	(87) Special activity loose equipment	(97)
(18) Other sub-structure elements	(28) Building frames, other primary elements	(38) Other secondary elements	(48) Other finishes to structure	(58) Other piped, ducted services	(68) Security, control, other services	(78) Other fittings	(88) Other equipment	(98) Other elements
(19) Parts of (11) to (19), cost summary	(29) Parts of (21) to (29), cost summary	(39) Parts of (31) to (39), cost summary	(49) Parts of (41) to (49), cost summary	(59) Parts of (51) to (59), cost summary	(69) Parts of (61) to (69), cost summary	(79) Parts of (71) to (79), cost summary	(89) Parts of (81) to (89), cost summary	(99) Parts of (91) to (99), cost summary

2 Types of drawing

2.1 Example of what can happen if site elements are not fully related. The manhole cover relates to neither the paving slabs nor the brick pavings

The types of drawings which make up the complete set having now been identified, this chapter looks at them in sequence to see the sort of information that each should contain.

The location drawing
The drawings falling into this category will normally include:
- site plan
- floor plans at all levels
- reflected ceiling plan at all levels
- roof plan
- foundation plan
- external elevations
- general sections and/or sectional elevations
- location sections.

Site plan
The functions of the site plan are to show:

> The location of the building (or buildings) in relation to its surroundings.
> The topography of the site, with both existing and finished levels.
> Buildings to be demolished or removed.
> The extent of earthworks, including cutting and filling, and the provision of banks and retaining walls.
> Roads, footpaths, hardstandings and paved areas.
> Planting.
> The layout of external service runs, including drainage, water, gas, electricity, telephone etc.
> The layout of external lighting.
> Fencing, walls and gates.
> The location of miscellaneous external components—bollards, litter bins, etc.

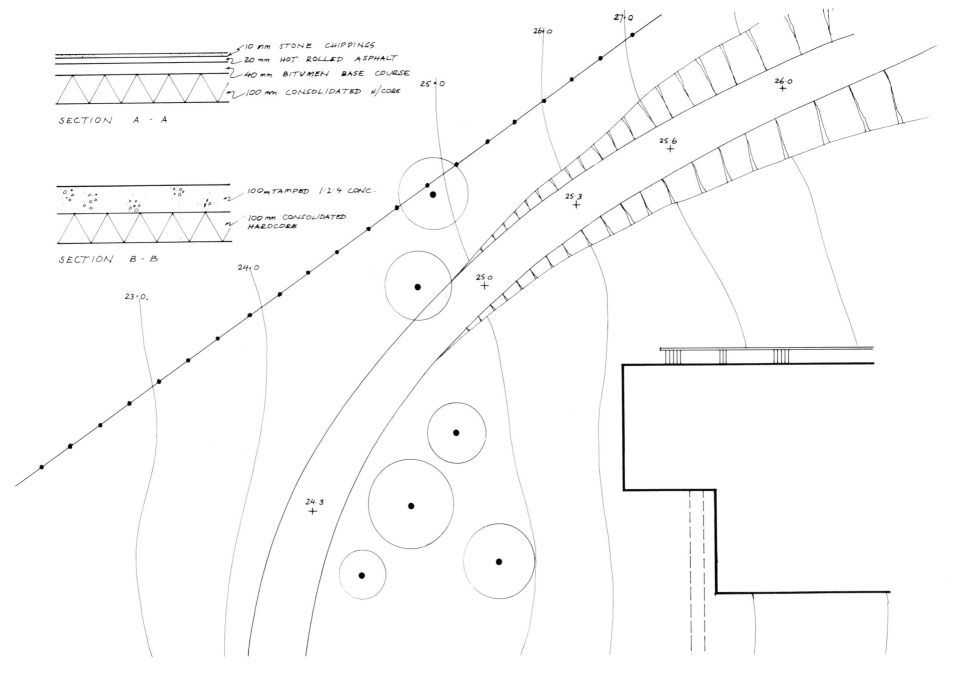

2.2 *Site plan with inset assembly details is not to be recommended. Such details form no part of what is essentially a location drawing*

These are multifarious functions, and some consideration has to be given to the desirability of elementalising them on to different drawings. The problem with site plans, however, is that these functions are closely interrelated. Incoming services may well share duct runs, if not the ducts themselves, which in turn will probably be related to the road or footpath systems; manhole covers will need to be related to paving layouts if an untidy and unplanned appearance is not to result (**2.1**).

There is a case for recording demolitions and earth-movement on separate drawings. These are after all self-contained activities which will precede the other site works. Indeed, they may well form the subject of separate contracts, and will often be carried out before other aspects of the site works have been finalised. Similarly, pavings—and more especially planting—are finishing elements which may benefit from separation. The remaining site works, however, are best recorded on a single drawing, and if problems of clarity and legibility seem likely to arise by virtue of the work being complicated, then the solution lies in producing the drawing at an appropriately generous scale rather than in attempting to fragment the information.

Most site plans that are unduly cluttered and difficult to read suffer from two faults:

1. They are drawn at too small a scale for the information they are required to carry.

2. They attempt to include detailed information—large scale details of road construction are a frequent example—which apart from crowding the sheet would more logically appear separately among the assembly information of which they clearly form part.

Figure **2.2** is a good example of how not to do it. There is clearly no room for the extraneous assembly information on what should be regarded solely as a location drawing, and it is interesting to speculate on the reasoning that led to it being there. In most cases, it appears for one of two reasons. The first is that the detail was an afterthought, and since no provision had been made for its inclusion elsewhere in the set, it seemed providential that the site plan had this bit of space in one corner. The second arises in the belief that it helps the builder to have everything on the one sheet.

This latter misconception extends over a much wider field of building communication than the site plan, and it cannot be refuted too strongly. *No* single document can ever be made to hold all the information necessary to define a single building element, let alone an entire building. If to place the assembly section of the road on the same sheet as its plan layout was deemed to be helpful in this instance, then why not the specification of the asphalt and the dimensions of the concrete kerb as well? The road cannot be constructed, or indeed priced by an estimator, without them. The essential art in building documentation is not the pursuit of a demonstrably mythical complete and perfect drawing, but the provision of a logical search pattern which will enable the user to find and assemble all the relevant information rapidly and comprehensively.

Figure **2.3**—taken from part of the site plan for a complex of buildings—illustrates some of the points made above.

Floor plans
There are three situations to consider:

- The location drawing designed to show a single building element, and what it should contain.

- The location drawing designed to be complete in itself—ie a drawing which in CI/SfB table 1 terminology would be described as 'The project in general' and coded (– –). (Clearly this type of drawing would only arise on the smallest and simplest of projects.)

- The basic location drawing, the drawing which provides the fundamental and minimal information which will appear as the framework for each individual elemental plan—the basic negative, in fact, from which future copy negatives containing elemental information will be taken.

Since the latter has a substantial bearing on the other two, it will be dealt with first.

The basic floor plan: Let us assume that you are to prepare a set of working drawings for a building project and that, by means of techniques to be discussed in a later chapter, you have decided that the floor plans will be elementalised in the following manner:

 (2–) Primary elements
 (3–) Secondary elements
 (5–) Services (piped and ducted)
 (6–) Services (electrical)
 (7–) Fittings.

Unless you are wildly profligate, masochistic, or an addictive draughtsman, you will not wish to draw each floor plan five times.

You will no doubt consider what common features of the plan will need to appear in all five drawings, with a view to drawing them once only as a master—or basic—sheet and taking five copy negatives from this master for subsequent elaboration into the respective elemental drawings.

You are thus faced with a decision of some nicety.

If you draw less than this common minimum on your basic negative you will be faced with a five-fold repair of your omission in due course. If you draw more than the minimum you will need to erase the surplus from subsequent copy negatives, or allow them to carry superfluous and possibly misleading information.

It is clearly important that the information carried by the basic negative, like the amount of lather specified in the old shaving soap advertisement, shall be not too little, not too much, but just right. See below for a check list of what this drawing should contain, and a list of those items which more often than not get added to the original needlessly and superfluously, to the subsequent inconvenience of everyone.

WORKING DRAWINGS HANDBOOK

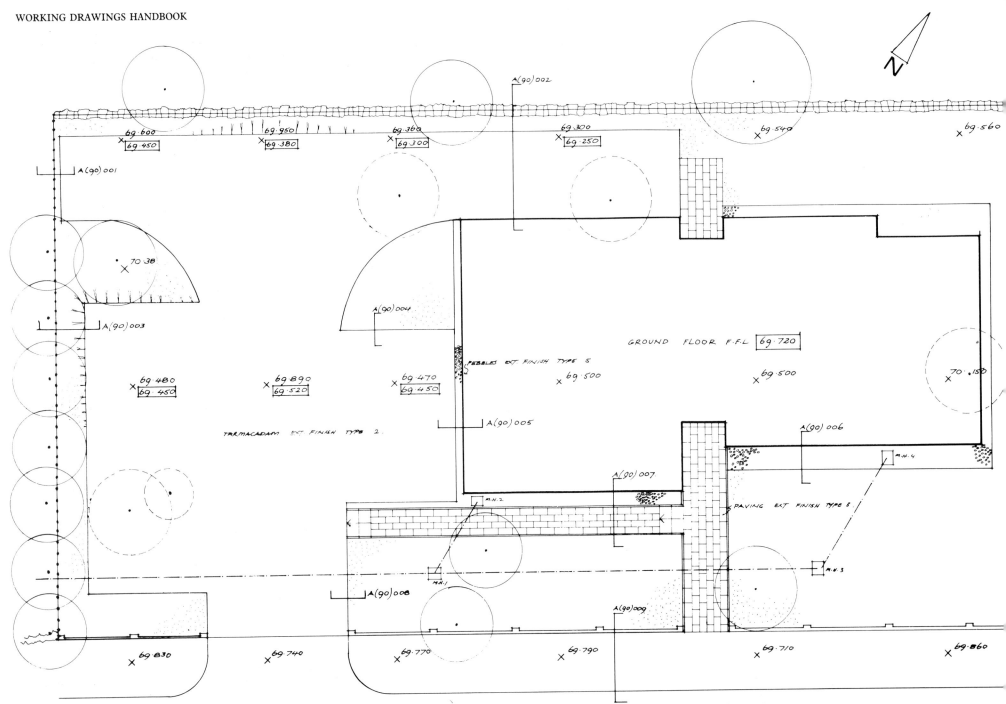

2.3 *A typical site plan. Information is given about new and existing levels and about paved surfaces, as well as directions as to where other information may be found*

TYPES OF DRAWING

To be included:
- Walls
- Main openings in walls (ie doors and windows)
- Partitions
- Main openings in partitions (doors)
- Door swings
- Room names and numbers
- Grid references (when applicable)
- Stairs (in outline)
- Fixed furniture (including loose furniture where its disposition in a room is in practice predetermined—eg desks set out on a modular grid etc)
- Sanitary fittings
- Cupboards
- North point.

Items which tend to be included but should not be:
- Dimensions
- Annotation
- Details of construction—eg cavity wall construction
- Hatching or shading
- Loose furniture where its disposition is not predetermined
- Section indications.

Figure **2.4** gives an idea of what should be aimed at. Note that a uniform line thickness is used throughout, and that this is the middle of the three line thicknesses which will be recommended in chapter 3. (Only the furniture carries a lesser weight of line in recognition of its non-building status.)

It is not the function of the basic drawing to differentiate between different elements, or to give differing values to them by graphical means. This will be done on the elemental drawings when emphasis may be given to the appropriate element by thickening the relevant lines.

The elemental floor plan: Generally speaking, if a project needs to be dealt with elementally then it will need to be separated into most or all of the following:

> (2–) Primary elements
> (3–) Secondary elements—possibly sub-divided into:
>   (35) suspended ceilings
> (4–) Finishes—possibly sub-divided into:
>   (42) internal finishes
>   (43) floor finishes
>   (45) ceiling finishes
> *(5–) Services—possibly sub-divided into any or all of the various constituent services
> *(6–) Installations—possibly sub-divided into:
>   (62) power
>   (63) lighting
>   (64) communications
> (7–) Fixtures
> (8–) Loose equipment.
>
> * Likely to be produced by other than the architect.

In other words, the breakdown is into the primary facets of CI/SfB table 1, and only in one or two special instances is it sometimes necessary to go any deeper. The reasons for this are apparent from a common-sense appraisal of the reason for elementalising the location plans in the first place—the desire to produce simple uncluttered drawings upon which different types of information will not be laid illegibly and confusingly one upon the other. If you consider the possible sub-divisions of the primary element facet it will be apparent that any drawn or annotated information about (21) external walls is unlikely to conflict with information about (22) internal walls or (23) floor construction. The different elements are physically separated on the drawing, and complete legibility may be maintained even though they share the same sheet of paper. Similarly (31) external openings are unlikely to conflict with (32) internal openings, and both may appear on the same drawing under the generic coding of (3–).

The problems begin to arise when it comes to ceilings, services and finishes. Some consideration must be given to the best method of documenting these, for boundaries tend to overlap and clear thinking is essential.

With regard to finishes, the practice of using a single floor plan to indicate wall, floor and ceiling finishes is not to be recommended. It is impossible for the plan to give detailed enough information about finishes to walls or elements associated with the walls without exhaustive (and exhausting) annotation, and systems of coded reference back to a written schedule tend to become elaborate and confusing (**2.5**).

Non-graphical room-by-room scheduling is a more satisfactory alternative. It is easy to produce and to refer to, and a lot of information may be conveyed by it. It has its disadvantages, the main one being the difficulty of relating the written description to an actual wall area or door surface but on the whole it is a reasonably effective method (**2.6**).

Of course, a description such as 'Two coats of emulsion' is helpful only to the estimator. Ultimately, somebody is going to ask 'what colour?' and a method of documentation which does not offer facilities for telling him concisely (let alone the possibility of explaining that you want the chimney breast in a different colour from the rest of the room) is an ill-considered one. So while there is a case to be made for including in the set a plan coded (43) and dealing solely with floor finishes (which will serve as a base drawing for dealing with nominated suppliers), finishes pertaining to walls and their ancillaries are best dealt with by a series of internal elevation sheets covering the whole project on a room-by-room basis.

Figure **2.7** shows a workable format for this, and demonstrates its use in positioning accurately those miscellaneous items which if otherwise unco-ordinated are apt to make an unexpected and unwelcome visual impact during a site visit late in the contract.

WORKING DRAWINGS HANDBOOK

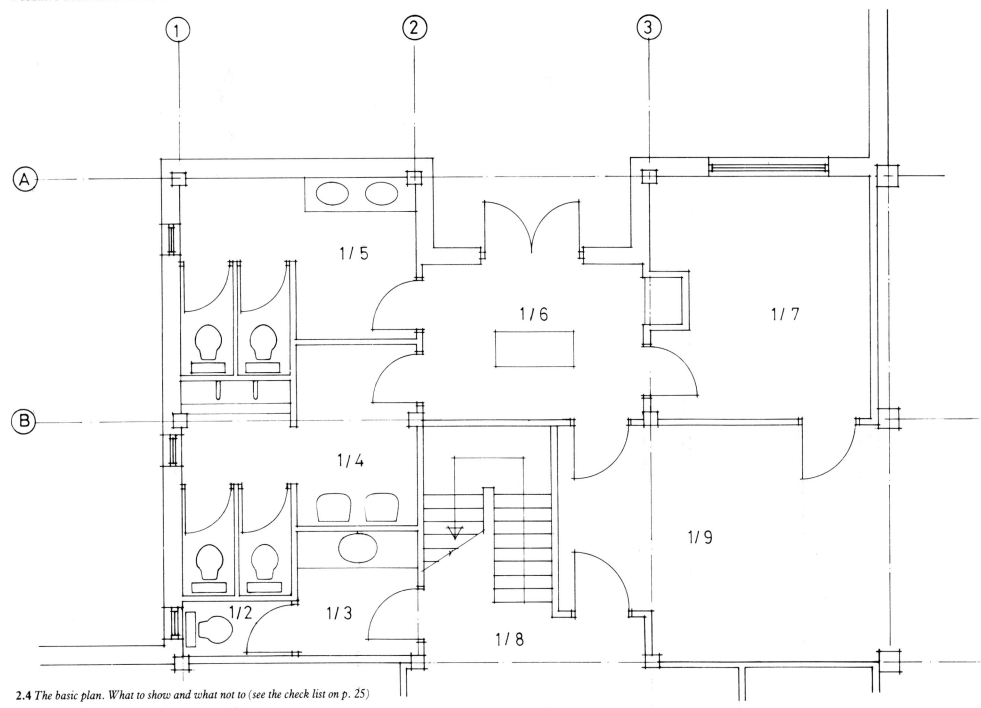

2.4 *The basic plan. What to show and what not to (see the check list on p. 25)*

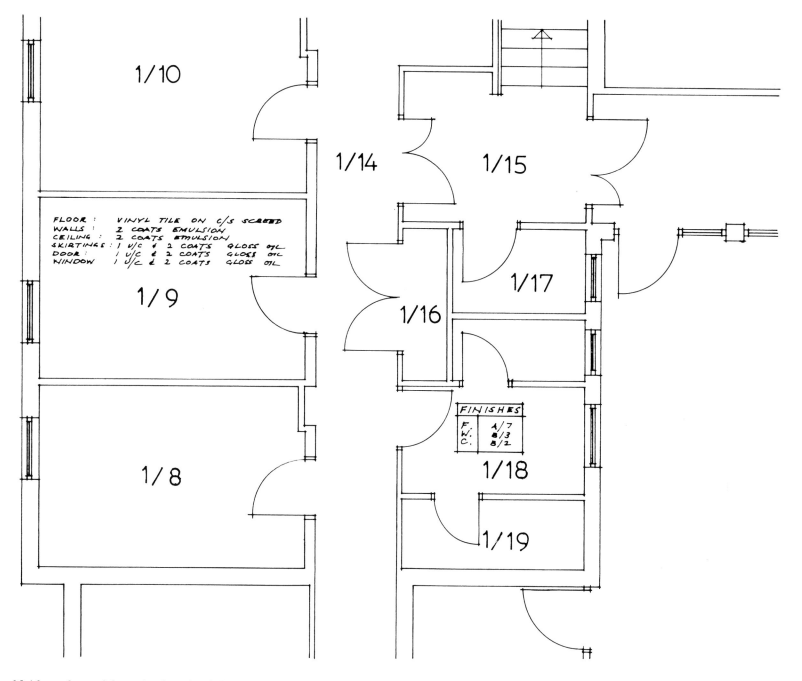

2.5 *Coded systems of finishes and over-elaborated written description on plans tend to be confusing*

ROOM NAME			ROOM NO.	
ELEMENT		FINISH	SPEC. CLAUSE NO.	COLOUR
FLOOR				
SKIRTING				
HEATER				
WALLS	1			
	2			
	3			
	4			
COLUMNS				
CILLS				
WINDOWS				
DOORS				
FRAMES				
CEILING				
FITTINGS				
WALL NOS. (1,2,3,4)	NOTES		A	
			B	
			C	
			D	
			E	

2.6 *Finishes given in schedule form. Strong on descriptive detail though weak on actual location, it nevertheless offers a simple and effective method*

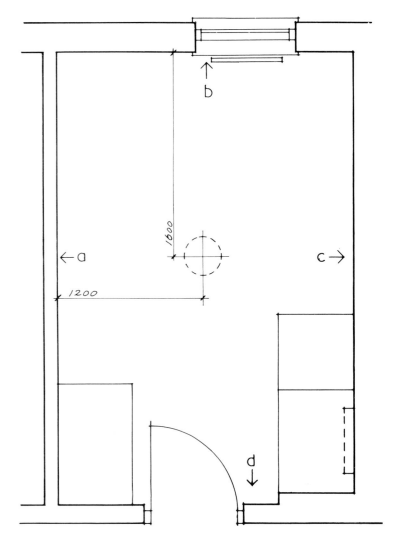

PLAN: ROOMS G/3 G/5 G/19 G/21
NOTE:- ROOMS G/4 G/6 G/20 & G/22 SIMILAR BUT OPP. HAND.

2.7 (*Above and facing page*) *Internal elevations on a room-by-room basis offer most flexible method for conveying information on finishes (scale of original 1:20)*

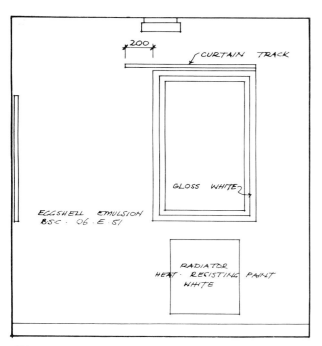

ELEVATION B.

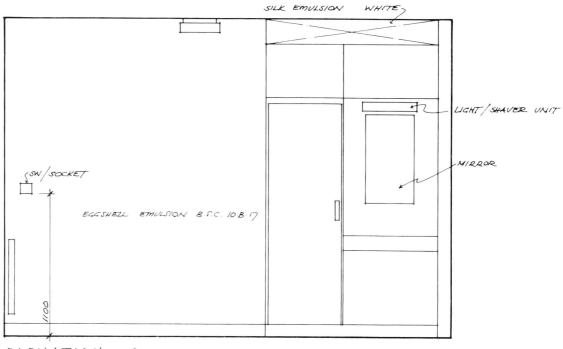

ELEVATION C.

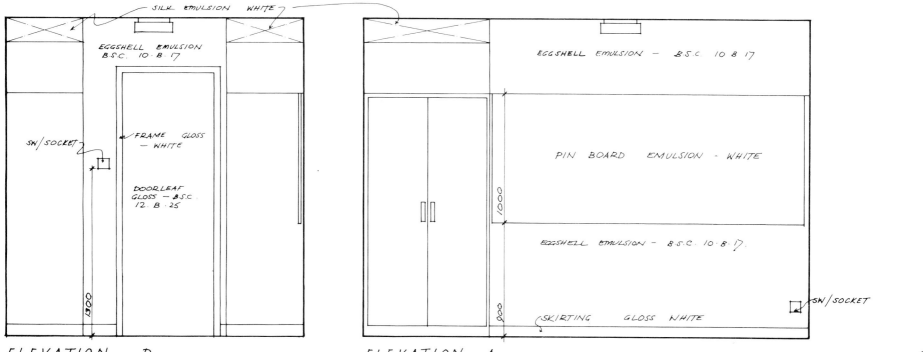

ELEVATION D.

ELEVATION A.

This leaves ceiling finishes to complete the room, but before simply opting for a (45) coded reflected ceiling plan the implications must be considered of any suspended ceilings (which CI/SfB table 1 would have us code (35)) and of the lighting and air-conditioning layouts, both of which will normally have a bearing on the ceilings.

Let us be clear about what we are trying to achieve. There will be a location plan of air-conditioning trunking—no doubt prepared by the M & E engineer—and coded, if the stage has been reached of having other consultants working within a CI/SfB format, L (57). There will also be a lighting layout, sprinkler layout, etc and each will also be a location drawing of the appropriate code reference. Should a drawing be produced to consolidate these various services, to ensure that they can co-exist satisfactorily in the same underfloor void, then it would be an assembly drawing, and sensibly coded A(5–), since the services as a whole are its primary concern. But at the end of the day the architect's final drawing must be of the ceiling *per se,* so that the precise positioning of diffusers, lighting fittings, sprinkler heads, etc may be visually acceptable, and may be taken to represent the 'picture on the lid' for all concerned with the construction of it. This is in every sense a location drawing and a finishes drawing, and it will be coded L(45). It completes the sixth side of the cube for every room on that particular floor level.

Figures **2.8, 2.9, 2.10** and **2.11** show how the various disciplines concerned have dealt with their respective layouts for a particular area, and how the L(45) ceiling finishes drawing serves as the picture of the finished product, as well as providing a useful vehicle for information about applied finishes which it would have been difficult to provide in any other way.

Roofs—particularly if they are flat roofs—are essentially just another floor, and it may be thought pedantic to introduce separate codes for them. Admittedly quantity surveyors and others concerned with elemental cost analysis require the distinction, but drawing codes do not always help here. Is **2.12** a roof plan of the factory, for instance, or is it a floor plan of the tank room?

On the whole it is preferable, in the interests of a coherent drawing package, to treat all horizontal divisions of the building as neither floors nor roofs but simply as 'levels', but to code them, when this becomes necessary, as floors.

This method has the inbuilt (and, on a large project, the very important) advantage that every plan level lies in a numerical sequence, and that in consequence (if care is taken) location plans of any one level, no matter what their elemental subject, will possess the same number.

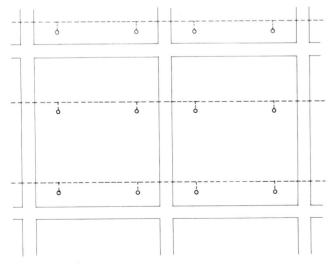

2.8 *Electrical layout at ceiling level*

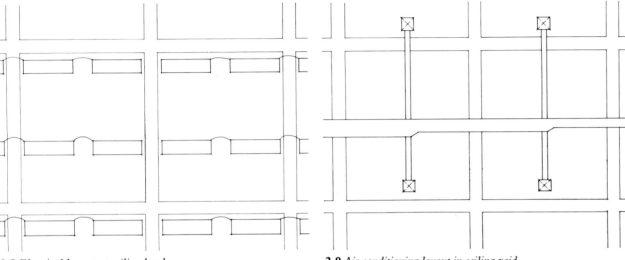

2.9 *Air conditioning layout in ceiling void*

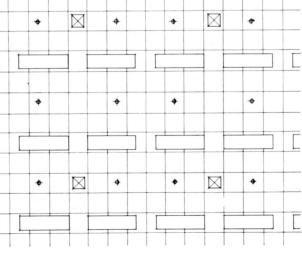

2.10 *Sprinkler layout at ceiling level*

2.11 *Architect's location drawing of the ceiling finishes provides co-ordinated layout for everyone involved*

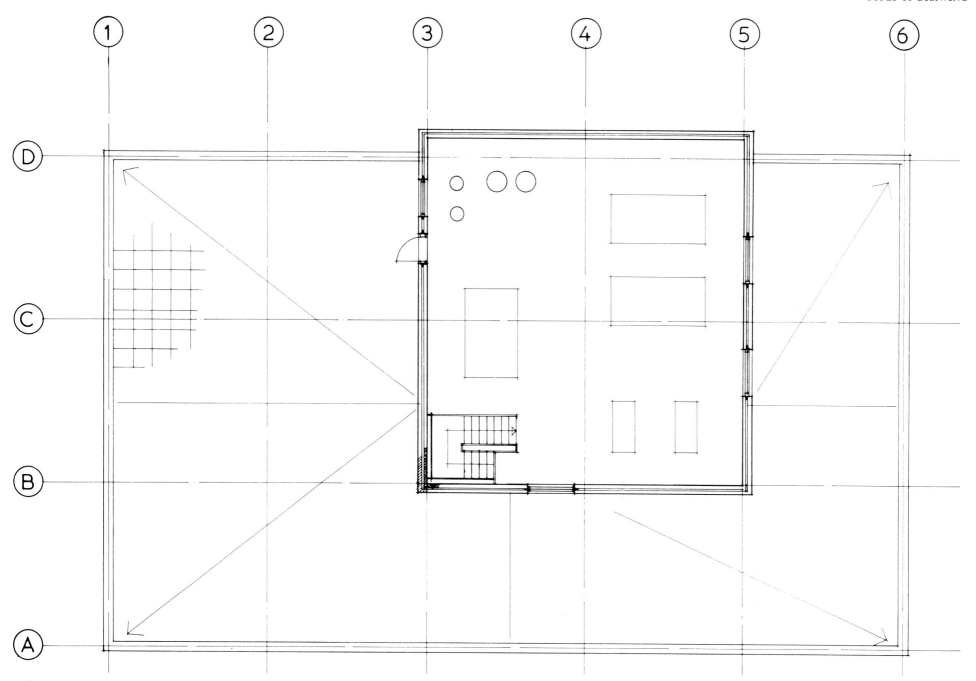

2.12 *Floor plan or roof plan? The problem is avoided if all plans are treated as 'levels'*

The elementalised location plans of level 3, for example, could be numbered:

L (2–) 003
L (3–) 003
L (42) 003
L (43) 003
L (45) 003 etc.

On a large project this is of immense practical importance to users of the drawing package because it offers them two ready sortations of the information. It is only necessary to assemble all the L (43) drawings, for example, to have the complete location information on floor finishes for the entire project. Assembly of all location drawings whose number is 003 on the other hand provides every elementalised location plan for level 3.

Some examples
It has already been noted that even the most complex of projects is unlikely to engage more than a handful of the available elemental sub-divisions. By the same token, it would be a very simple project indeed that did not benefit from some degree of elementalisation. The examples given here—taken from the drawing set whose basic location plan was shown in **2.4**—cover some of the most fundamental sub-divisions, those dealing respectively with primary and secondary elements.

Location plans—Primary elements Note that CI/SfB table 1 offers the following choice within the general summary code (2–):

```
(21) Walls, external walls
(22) Internal walls, partitions
(23) Floors, galleries
(24) Stairs, ramps
(27) Roofs
(28) Building frames, other primary elements.
```

In the project illustrated (**2.13**) the decision was made to confine the architect's information about primary elements to a single, (2–) drawing. A similar decision was made at about the same time in relation to a smaller and simpler project. Since the reasons for arriving at this decision were different in each case, they serve to illustrate the importance of thinking about what you are trying to achieve before actually starting to draw.

On the larger of the two projects, which had a reinforced concrete frame and floor slabs, and which enjoyed the services of a structural consultant, it was deemed unnecessary, not to say inadvisable, for the architect's drawings to give constructional information about structural elements which were clearly the responsibility of the structural engineer. So floors (23), stairs (24), roofs (27) and frames (28), whilst appearing on the architect's primary element drawing (for they appeared in outline on the basic negative in which these elementalised plans had their origin) nevertheless remain in outline only. Against each of these elements appears a reference to the fact that the appropriate structural engineer's drawing should be consulted, thus satisfying the second of the two basic functions of a location plan—either to locate the element it deals with, or to state where its location may be found.

Of the other primary elements—and in this particular example the walls and partitions are the primary consideration—the information given about them consists of statements as to where they are to be placed (ie dimensions from known reference points—sensibly, in this instance, the structural grid); what they consist of (ie notes on their materials, or reference back to more detailed specification information); and where further information about them may be found (ie coded references to relevant assembly details). The primary elements dealt with on this particular drawing, as distinct from primary elements dealt with on other location drawings, are identified by being emphasised in a heavier line than that used for the rest of the drawing.

The comparable (2–) drawing for the smaller of the two projects had obvious points of similarity, but the reasoning behind its production was somewhat different. The building was of simple two-storeyed load-bearing brick construction, with simply supported timber roof and floor joists, and timber staircase. There was no structural engineer, so the design and detailing of these structural elements devolved upon the architect.

A case might be argued for separating the structural elements anyway, in which case the architect might have produced a set of primary element drawings consisting of floors (23) and roofs (27), with the other primary elements being incorporated in a summary (2–) sheet. But the modest size of this building meant that it could be drawn quite manageably (in this case on A2 sheets) at a scale of 1:50, and the generally more relaxed nature of the drawing at that scale meant that more information could be conveyed legibly than would have been the case had the size of the project necessitated the use of a scale of 1:100. So again a (2–) summary drawing sufficed for all the primary elements.

A point is worth making about the way in which the brickwork was described in each case, because it illustrates the fundamentally common-sense way in which all such decisions should be handled. In the larger building there were four different types of brickwork involved. These were:

1. A Class II engineering brick in cement mortar, used in manholes and certain works below ground.
2. A common brick to BS 3921 Part II, laid in a 1:1:6 mortar mix and used generally for all backings.
3. A sand-lime facing to BS 187, laid in 1:1:6 mortar to a Flemish bond, and used generally as a facing brick to wall panels.
4. A hand-made fired clay facing brick, used in certain featured areas on the entrance facade, and laid to a decorative pattern.

A schedule of brickwork types formed part of the specification, in which each type was fully identified and described. The reference Fg1/3 on the drawing indicates that it is the third type of brickwork in that schedule, which since the project included the National Building Specification as part of its documentation was to be

TYPES OF DRAWING

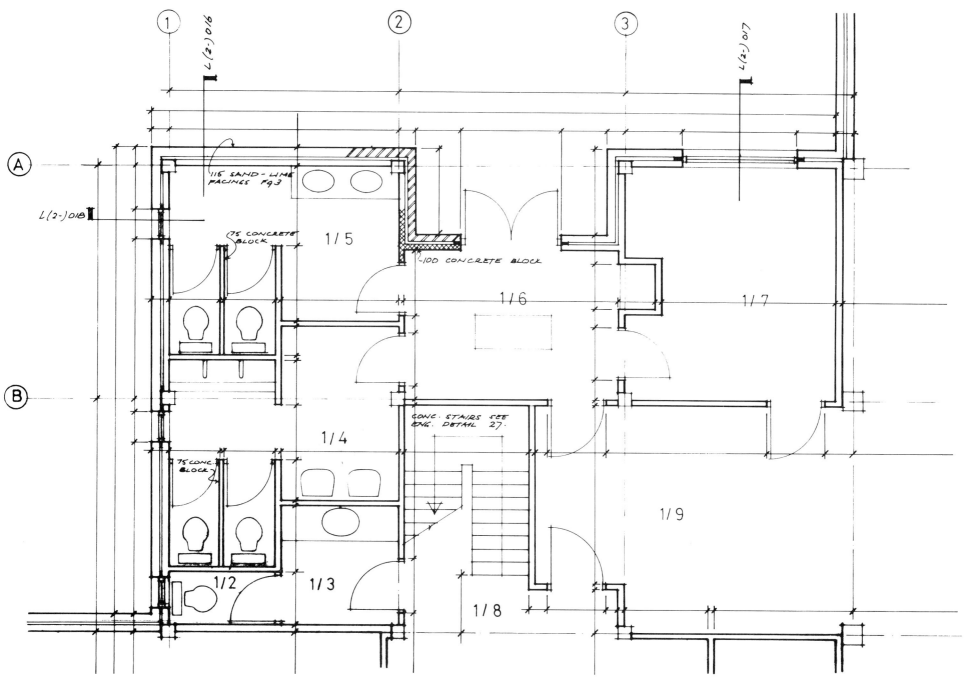

2.13 *Elemental plan showing primary (2-) elements*

WORKING DRAWINGS HANDBOOK

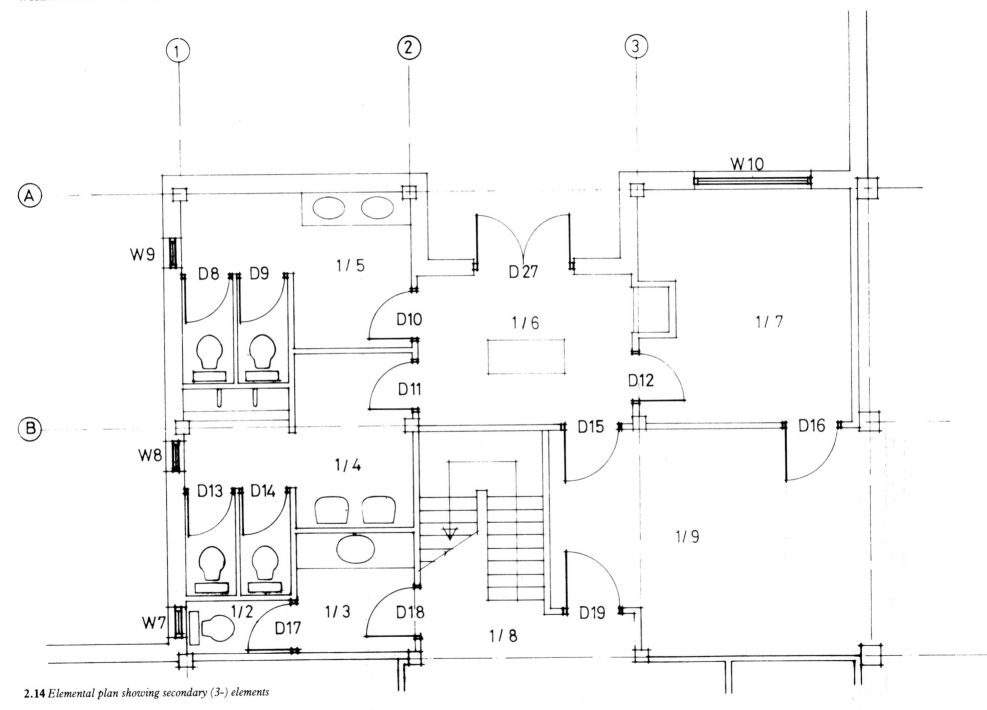

2.14 *Elemental plan showing secondary (3-) elements*

TYPES OF DRAWING

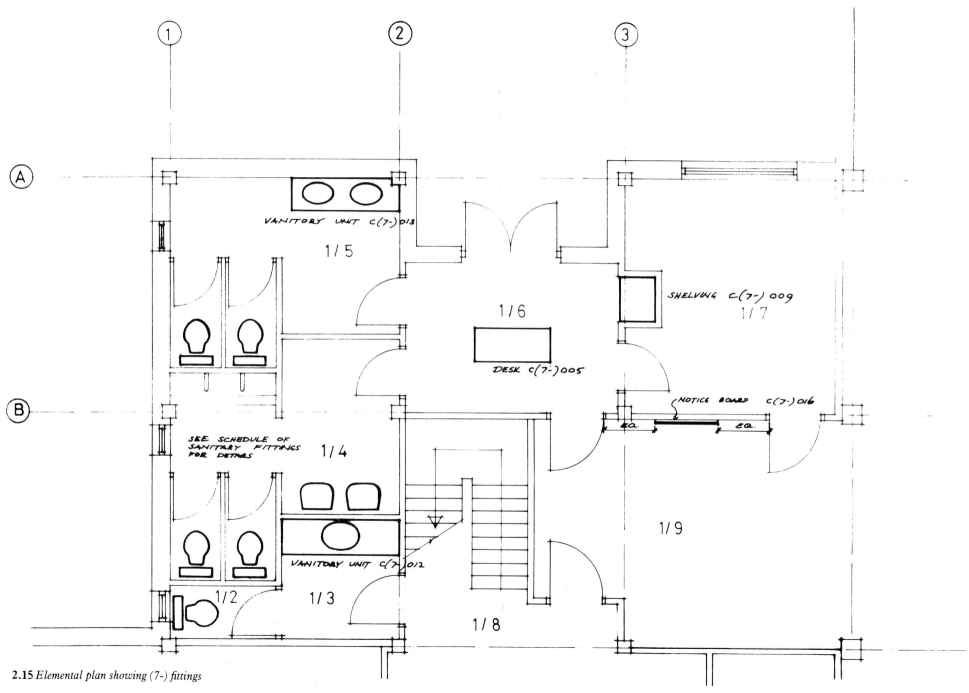

2.15 *Elemental plan showing (7-) fittings*

found in the Fg (bricks and blocks) section of that specification. 'Brickwork Type 3' would have been an equally specific identification.

On the smaller project, however, only two types of brick were used—a common brick and a facing brick. So, in this instance, the description 'facing brick'—assuming the specification has fulfilled its proper descriptive function—was perfectly adequate.

In neither case is it likely that the routine of the drawing office was disrupted a year later by someone telephoning from site to ask 'which brick goes here?'.

Location plans—secondary elements: Although produced from the same basic negative, the (3–) plan illustrated in **2.14** has, at first glance, almost the appearance of being a photographic negative reproduction of the corresponding (2–) plan illustrated previously. Where the earlier drawing showed the walls heavily lined, there is now the thinnest of indicative outlines. Where the (2–) plan left in outline the breaks in walls left for doors and windows we now have those breaks heavily framed to emphasise the components that are to fill them. As in the (2–) series, annotations and references to assembly drawings and scheduled information are confined to those elements which form the subject of the drawing.

The example in **2.16** illustrates the virtues of secondary structuring of drawings and the inherent flexibility of elementalisation when used with common sense and imagination. The project in question was one of a number dealing with a similar building type, each of which involved the appointment of a nominated sub-contractor for various shop-fitting works. With certain building elements—doors, pelmet and skirtings, for example—being carried out by the main contractor in some areas and by the shopfitter in others, it was important that the method of documentation employed should be capable of defining satisfactorily the limits of responsibility for each. It was also desirable that it should provide for separate packages of information being available upon which each could tender.

The method adopted in practice was to treat all the work of the shopfitter as a (7–) fittings element, regardless of rigid CI/SfB definitions, and to record it on a (7–) location plan, while the work of the main contractor appeared on separate location plans covering (2–) primary elements, (3–) secondary elements and (4–) finishes. Assembly drawings involving the work of both main contractor and shopfitter were referenced from all the relevant location plans, and were included in both packages of information.

Location plans—format: With very small buildings it is perhaps pedantic to ask that each of (two) plans be drawn on a separate piece of paper when both fit perfectly happily one above the other on a single A2 sheet. In general, however, it is desirable that each sheet should be devoted to one plan level only, the size of the building and the appropriate scale determining the basic size of sheet for the whole project.

Leave plenty of space on the sheet. Apart from the fact that this tends to get filled up by notes, etc during the course of the drawing's production (the addition of three strings of dimensions on each face alone adds considerably to the original plan area of the drawing), it must be remembered that the drawing's various users will in all probability wish to add their own notes to the prints in their possession.

Location elevations—external
Given the plan view and sufficient sections through an object, it is arguable that it is unnecessary to show it in elevation for the object to be fully comprehended. That so much often goes wrong on a building site, even with the benefit of elevations, is an illustration of the fact that the construction process often has little connection with formal logic; in practice to erect a building without a set of elevations is a little like trying to assemble a jig-saw puzzle without the picture on the lid to refer to from time to time.

Nevertheless, it is as well to remember that the elevation's function is primarily pictorial rather than informative, and that in consequence it should not be made to carry information more sensibly conveyed by other means.

If elevations are to be of relevance they must be complete, and this means not just the four views—front, back and two sides—that sometimes suffice, but sectional elevations covering re-entrant points in the plan shape and the elevations of courtyards.

Remember too that the building consists of more than that which can be seen above ground. One of the more useful aspects of a properly drawn set of elevations is that an indication can be given of the sub-structure, and of the building's relationship with the immediately surrounding terrain or pavings (**2.17**).

We have mentioned sectional elevations, and we may as well deal here with general sections also, for in this context they serve the same purpose as the elevations, in that they present a general picture of the building without necessarily providing any specific information from which it might be built. They are of particular value to the contractor when he is planning the sequence of his operations on site, and for this reason those items of particular relevance to this function—the relationships of floor levels to one another and of the building to the ground are obvious instances—must be shown adequately (**2.18**).

Elevations too should carry grid lines and finished floor levels. Other than that they should be simply drawn, with all visible features included but not unduly elaborated.

Windows in particular tend to be over-drawn; there is really no point in elaborating glazing bars and beads when these aspects are going to be covered much more fully on the appropriate component drawings. Brick courses merely confuse the eye. We are not dealing here with an artistic pictorial simulation of the building but with a schematic factual representation.

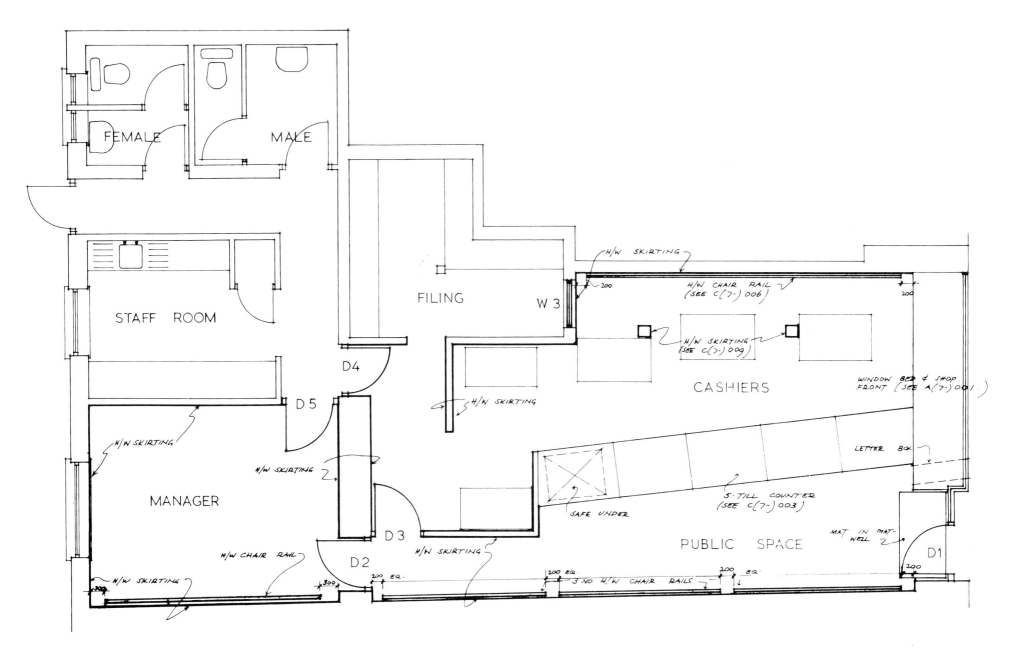

2.16 *Elementalisation used flexibly in practice. The (7–) location drawing shown gives a clear exposition of the responsibilities of one nominated sub-contractor – in this case the shopfitter*

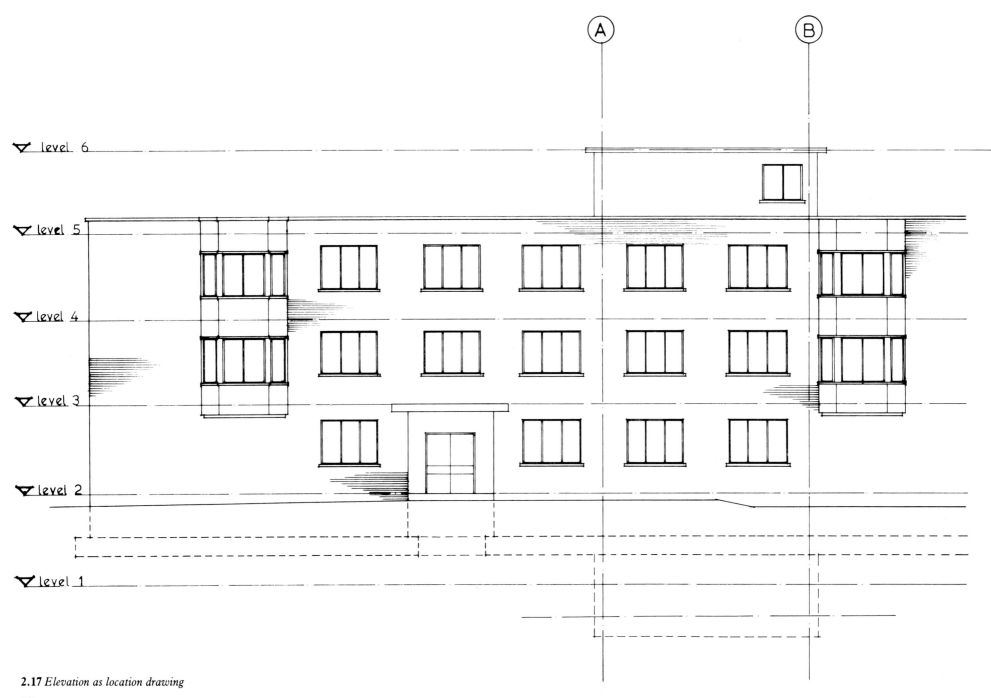

2.17 *Elevation as location drawing*

TYPES OF DRAWING

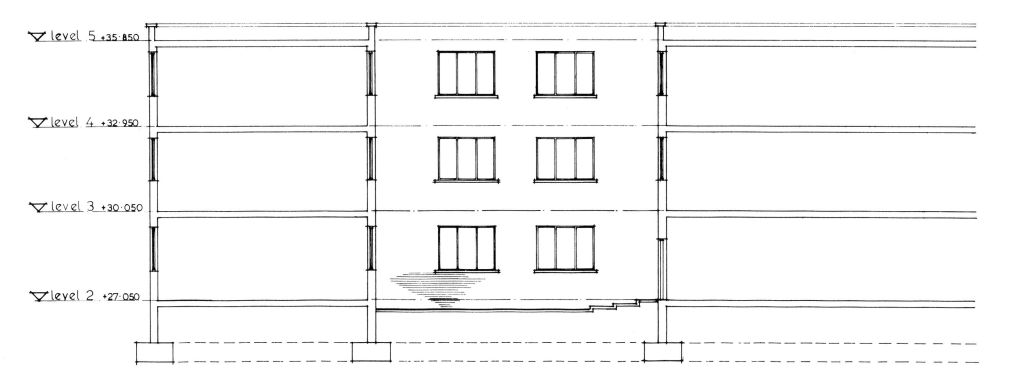

2.18 *Location sections—designed to convey a general indication of what the contractor may expect rather than a detailed instruction of what he is to build*

There are four areas where elementalisation of the elevations should be considered, particularly on larger projects:

1. They may be used to locate external openings, and this can be a helpful means of cross-reference back to the external openings schedule. All that is necessary is for the opening reference—(31)007, (31)029—to be written on the appropriate opening in elevation. The practice, sometimes attempted, of using the elevation as the actual external openings schedule is not to be recommended. More needs to be said about the average window than can sensibly be carried in a small box on a 1:200 elevation.

Such references are useful in relating a point on the elevation with its corresponding position on plan, but the elevation should never be regarded as the primary source of reference for these components. Regardless of whether or not they appear on the elevations, it is essential that the references appear on the appropriate location plans (**2.19**).

2. They may be used to identify the type and extent of external finishes, and this is a useful device, for it is not easy by any other means to indicate such things as patterned brickwork, the change from one type of bond or pointing to another, or soldier courses (**2.20**).

3. They may be used as both location drawings and schedule for cladding panels or ashlar facings (**2.21**).

4. They may be used to convey information about external plumbing and drainage services above ground (**2.22**).

When used elementally the same graphical considerations apply to elevations as have been mentioned already in the context of elementalised location plans.

Location sections

Location plans in effect constitute a series of horizontal cross-sections through the building, spaced out so that one is taken at every floor level. This spacing is reasonable, since in practice the appearance of the horizontal section is most likely to differ from floor to floor, and unlikely to differ between floor and ceiling.

If a series of comparable vertical cuts were made through the building, again taking a fresh one whenever the appearance of the section changed, the result would be a very large number of sections indeed. Such vertical sections constitute a vital aspect of the information to be conveyed, yet their number must be limited to manageable proportions.

Fortunately, a large proportion of the possible sections tell us very little about the building. Figure **2.23**, which reduces the cross-section through a multi-storeyed building to a diagrammatic simplicity, will explain why.

Most of it is irrelevant to our understanding. The internal elevations of those rooms which are exposed by the section cut are not a very suitable medium for describing, for example, wall finishes, since the other three walls of the room are not shown. It is true that we are shown the positions of doors in those walls, but these are shown, and indeed dimensioned, much more comprehensively on the respective floor plans.

The heights of internal door frames may be derived whenever the section line passes through an internal wall coincident with a door opening, but the height of the frame may be obtained more readily from the component drawing of the doorset of which it will form part.

The only pieces of information it carries which are not readily obtainable from other sources in fact, are the height of the window cill, the height of the parapet, the relative floor levels, and the thickness of the floor construction. Each of these items of information would be conveyed just as effectively if the section were confined to the narrow strip running through the external walls (**2.24**).

Since the number of potentially different wall sections will be limited, the vast number of separate cross-sectional cuts through the building at first envisaged is reduced to manageable proportions. Those strip sections may also be used as a reference point for the detailed construction information which needs to be given about window head, window cill, parapet, footings and the junctions of floors with walls, and as such they may be regarded as forming part of the location information for the project.

There is little point in attempting to use the strip sections themselves to convey this detailed information unless the building is so small, or so simple in its design, that a few such sections tell all that needs to be conveyed about the construction. In most instances the scale of the section, and the number of times it will change around the building, will make it more sensible to treat the location section in almost diagrammatic terms.

Note that the floor levels are given, and that the vertical dimensions (for example, to window cills) are given from those floor levels to a datum (for example, the top of the last course of bricks) which is readily achievable on site, and to which the more comprehensive dimensioning contained in the subsequent details may be referred.

There is no advantage in elementalising the location sections, although if CI/SfB coding is being used there is some advantage in regarding them as L (2–) drawings, thus differentiating them from the L (– –) general sections previously described and which fulfil a different purpose in the set.

The points around the building at which the strip sections are taken will, of course, be indicated on the location plans (**2.25**).

Component drawings

A component may be defined as any item used in a building which emanates from a single source of supply and which arrives on site as a complete and self-contained unit, whose incorporation into the building requires only its fixing to another component or components. Thus, a window is clearly a component, as is a manhole cover, a door, a section of pre-cast

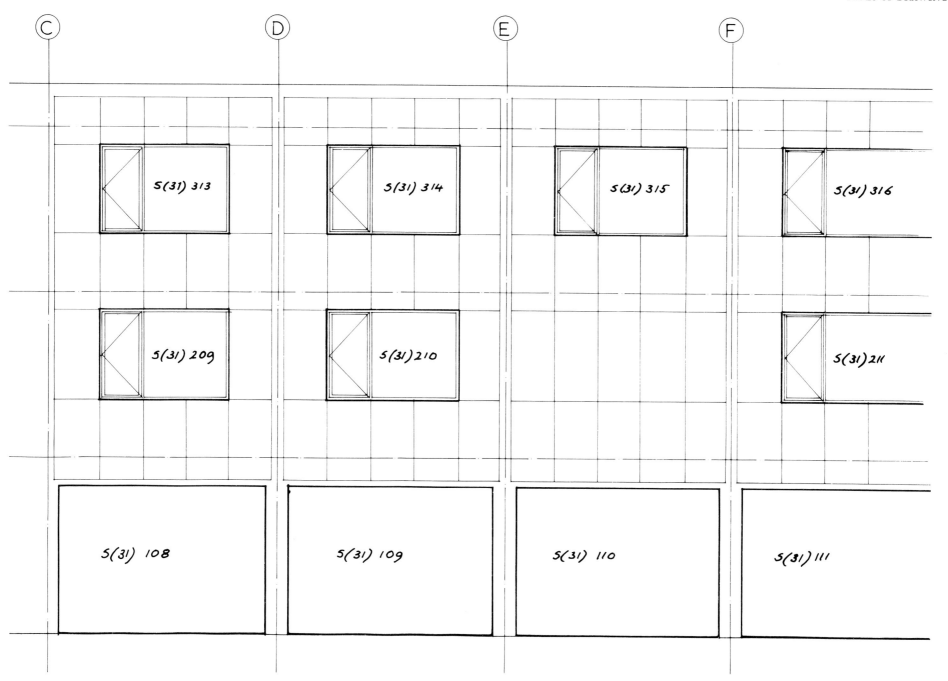

2.19 *Elevation as a secondary reference to window components. The reference 'S(31) –' leads back to the external wall secondary elements schedule where the components are listed and classified*

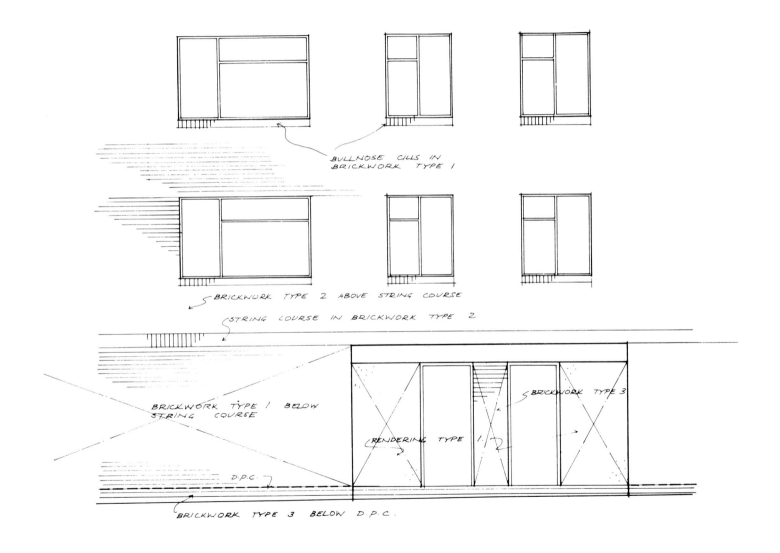

2.20 *Elevation as a guide to external finishes not easily indicated in detail by other means*

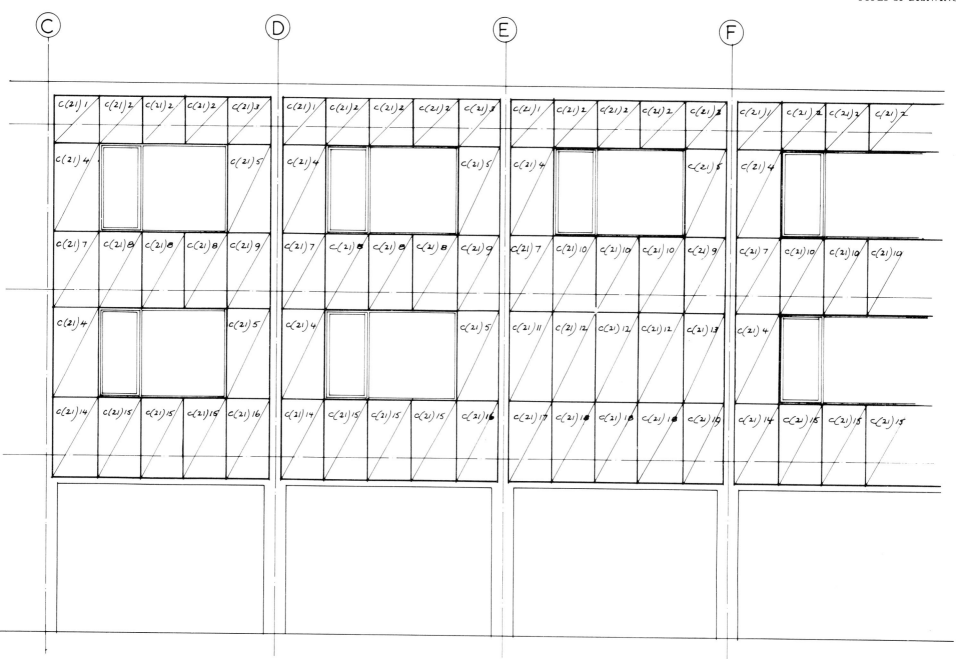

2.21 *Elevation as a schedule for pre-cast panels. Note the difference in method from that used in 2.19. Here, with a limited range of panel types, and with each panel component drawing giving full information about it, the elevation itself forms an adequate schedule*

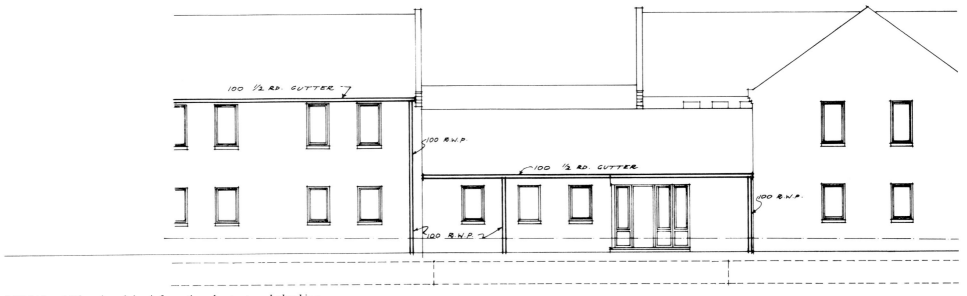

2.22 (Above) Elevation giving information about external plumbing

2.23 (Facing page) Diagrammatic cross-section through a multi-storeyed building. Virtually all the information it gives may be conveyed more fully and intelligibly by other means – the frames will be built from the structural engineer's drawings; the doors will be manufactured from information to which the joiner is directed from the appropriate schedules, and will be installed in positions given on the floor plans; the construction of the external walls will be found on strip sections amplified as necessary by larger scale details. A cross-section such as that shown has its functions, but they are likely to be advisory – i.e. letting the contractor see the sort of building he is embarking upon – rather than directly instructing him what to build and where to build it

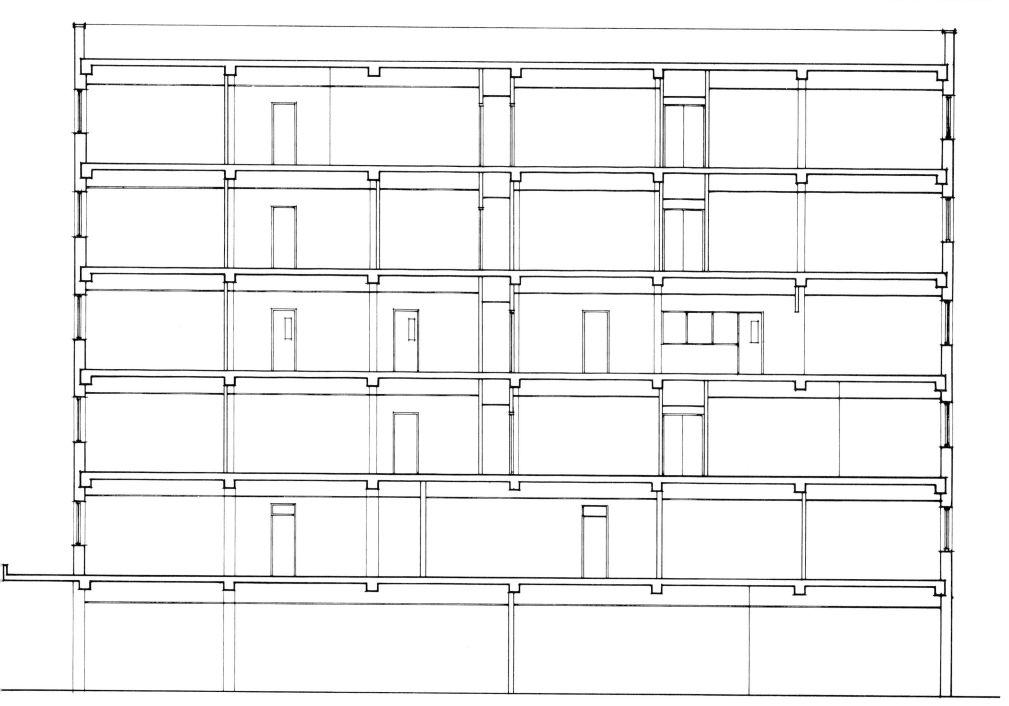

concrete coping, a mirror. So, for that matter, is a brick. (A brick wall would be an assembly.)

Two types of component should be distinguished:

1. There is the manufacturer's product, available off the builders' merchants' shelf, for which no descriptive drawing need be prepared. Such items as standard windows, sanitary fittings and proprietary kitchen units may be described uniquely by the quotation of a catalogue reference. If they are to be drawn at all then their draughting will be in the simplest terms, more for the avoidance of doubt in the minds of architect and contractor than for any other reason. Certainly any detail as to their method of construction will be at best redundant, and at worst highly amusing to the manufacturer.
2. There is the special item requiring fabrication—the non-standard timber window, the reception desk, the pre-cast concrete cladding panel—and in order that someone may make it as required, it is necessary for the architect to define quite precisely what it is he wants, and (in many instances) how he wants it to be made.

Clearly it is the latter category that is of most concern at the drawing stage.

In both categories, however, a basic principle holds good. The component in question should always be defined as the largest single recognisable unit within the supply of a particular manufacturer or tradesman. An example will make this clear.

Figure **2.26** shows an elevation of a row of fixed and opening lights, contained within a pre-cast concrete frame, and separated from each other by either a brick panel or a pressed metal mullion. How many window components are there? We may look at this in various ways, and all of them would have some logical force behind them. We could say, for example, that there were six window components of which four were of type A and two were of type B (see **2.27**). There is an attractive simplicity about this view.

It could be argued with equal justification, that we had in fact a single component, consisting of an assemblage of fixed lights, opening lights, coupling mullions and brick infill panels. The component, in fact, is everything held within the overall pre-cast concrete frame (see **2.28**). This approach too has its attractions.

The correct procedure, however, will be to regard the whole assembly as consisting of two window components (**2.29**).

The key determining factor here is the supply of the component. It is reasonable to make the window manufacturer responsible for supplying the pressed metal coupling mullions, but not for supplying the brick panel—and if he is to provide the coupling mullions, then it is rash and unnecessarily intrusive for the architect (inexperienced in this field) to take responsibility for the assembly junction between light and mullion. One of the problems associated with an increasingly factory-oriented building technology is ensuring a satisfactory fit when two components of different manufacture come together on site. Treating the component as embracing the coupling mullions at least puts one aspect of the problem squarely on the shoulders of the window manufacturer, who is best equipped to deal with it.

This principle may be extended with advantage. If doors and frames are treated as two separate components the responsibility becomes that of the architect to ensure that the door meets the frame with the correct tolerances. If, however, the component is regarded as being the complete doorset, then dimensional considerations apply only to the overall size of the frame, and it is the joiner who ensures that door and frame fit one another. This is not passing the buck. Rather, it is putting back in the right hands a buck which the architect should never have picked up in the first place.

It is, of course, part of the architect's professional responsibility to ensure that he does not specify overall

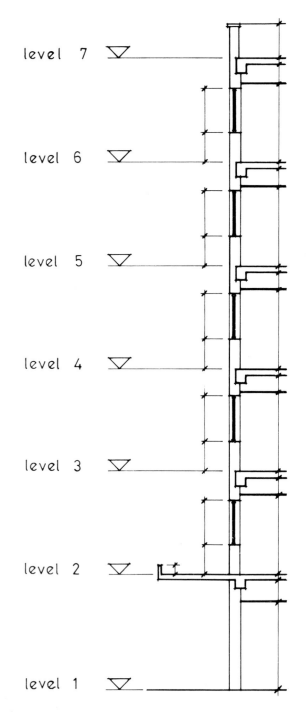

TYPES OF DRAWING

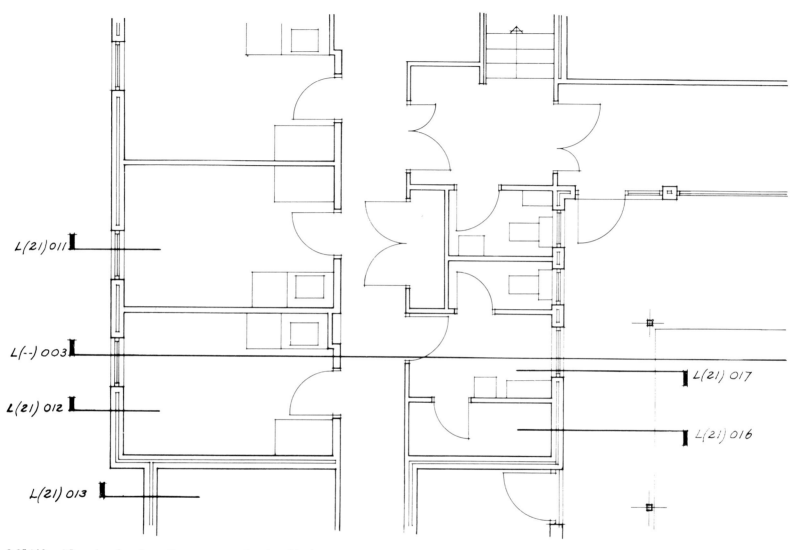

2.25 (Above) Location plan gives references to general sections L(--) and strip sections L(21). The former will be of the type shown in 2.23. The latter will be similar in scope and function to that shown in 2.24

2.24 (Left) Sectional cut confined to perimeter of building

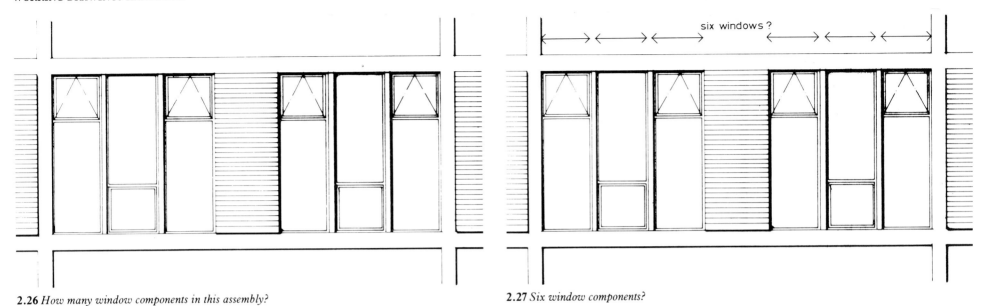

2.26 *How many window components in this assembly?*

2.27 *Six window components?*

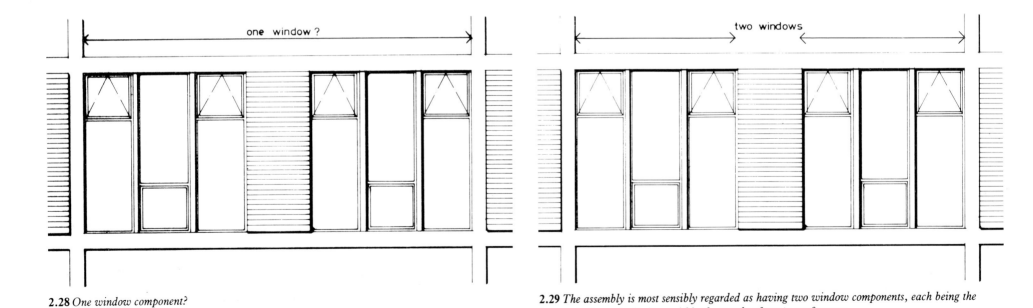

2.28 *One window component?*

2.29 *The assembly is most sensibly regarded as having two window components, each being the largest single composite item within the supply of one manufacturer* doorset sizes complete with frame dimensions which involve expensive non-standard doorleaf sizes. Similarly, he must have the basic technical knowledge of joinery production to ensure that he does not ask for a frame size which involves a third of the timber ending up as shavings on the joinery shop floor simply because the finished section was just too large to allow it to be run from a more economically-sized sawn baulk.

Refinements in documentation method may simplify the process of building communications, but they cannot serve as substitutes for fundamental technical knowledge. (See also the notes on co-ordinating dimensions and work-sizes in chapter 3.)

Format
Component drawings lend themselves to re-use within an office in a way that is unlikely to occur with other categories of drawing. They can, of course, always be transferred from one project to another by tracing, but one of the advantages of a comprehensive communications system is the facility it offers of standardising the format of such details, and hence enabling them to be transferred direct from one project to another without the necessity for re-drawing. The resultant benefits in economy and consistency are obvious (**2.30**). For this reason a standard format should be considered, and the drawing size will probably be smaller than that used for the rest of the project. (The merits of the different sizes available are discussed in chapter 3.)

Figures **2.31**, **2.32** and **2.33** show three typical examples of component drawing. It should be noted that the general rule whereby drawing and specification information are segregated may be relaxed with advantage in the case of components, particularly when, (as for example fig **2.33**) they form part of a standard office library.

Note also that in fig **2.32** the term 'component' has been extended to embrace the method of fixing as well as the description of what is to be fixed. It is only common

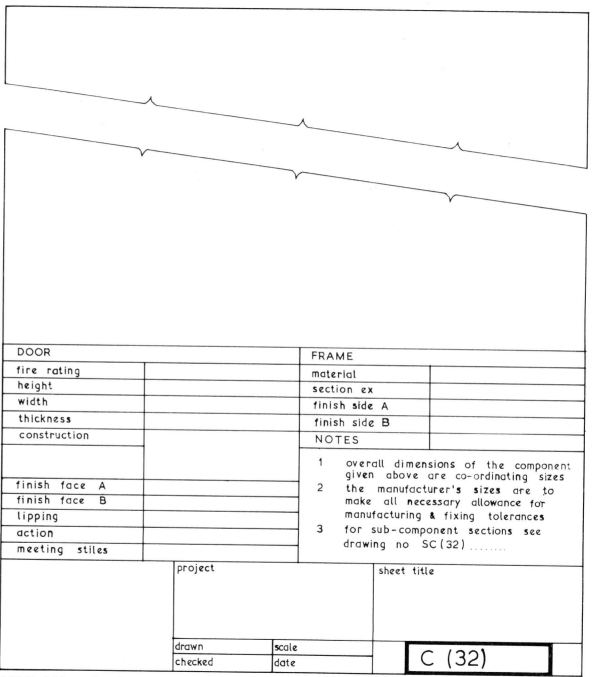

2.30 *Useful format for a door component drawing*

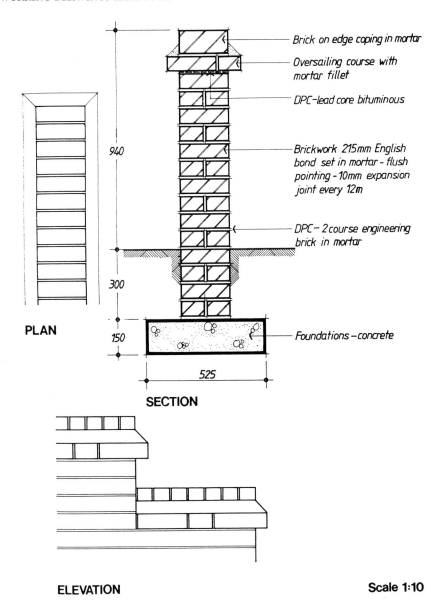

2.31 External works components such as this lend themselves to standardisation. (*Illustration from* Landscape Detailing *by Michael Littlewood, Architectural Press, London, 1984*)

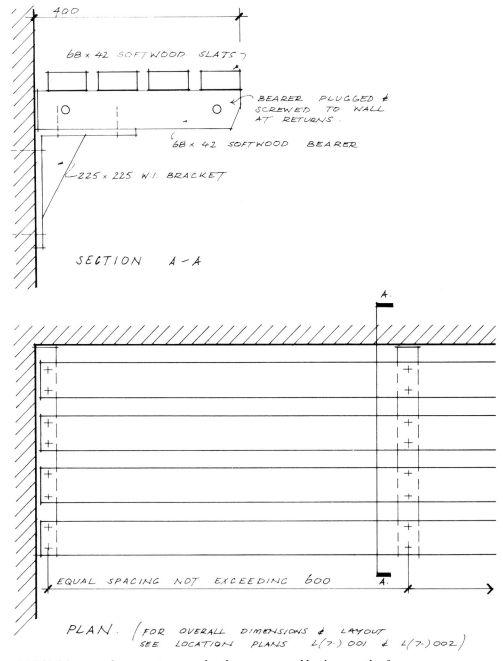

2.32 *Shelving treated as a component rather than as an assembly. An example of common sense overriding too rigid theories of classification*

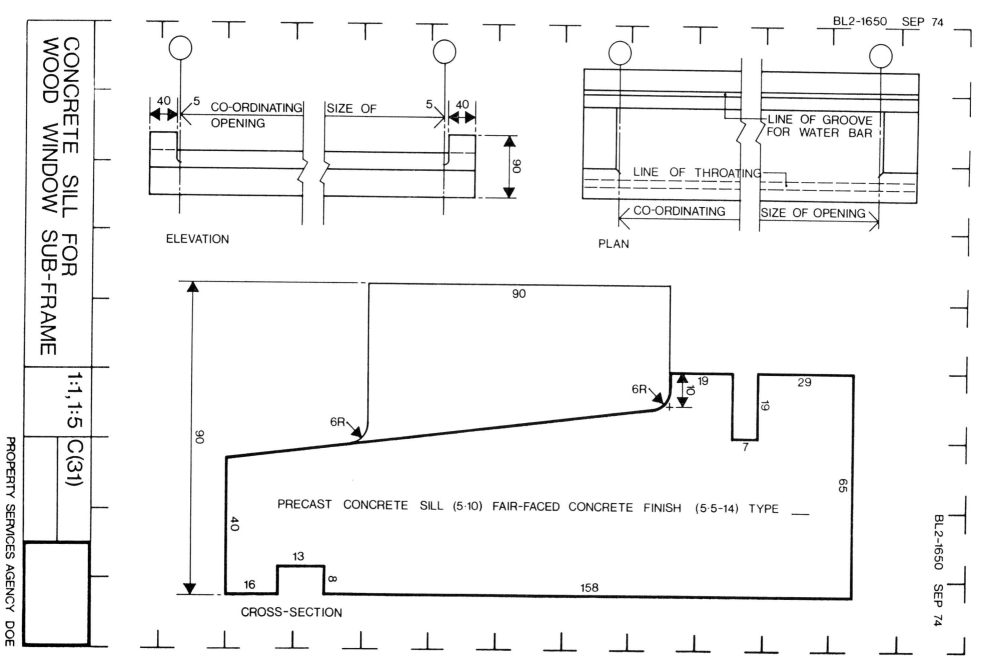

2.33 *Component detail of concrete cill*

WORKING DRAWINGS HANDBOOK

sense to treat such drawings as components rather than assemblies. Furthermore, the alternative fixing methods shown and the references back to the location drawings for overall sizes makes this one small detail of universal applicability when shelving of this nature is required throughout even the largest project.

Sub-component drawings
These have a limited use and often the information they convey will be better shown on the component drawing. There are instances, however, particularly when a range of components is being dealt with of which the sizes and appearance differ but the basic construction remains constant, when it may be more economical to present details of the construction on a separate drawing.

For example, **2.34** shows two doorsets of different sizes and different types. The basic sections from which they are fabricated are similar, however, and that fact has been acknowledged in this instance by the production of a sub-component drawing (**2.35**) to which the various component drawings refer.

The method is really best suited to large projects, or to those offices which have produced their own standard ranges of component details.

The assembly drawing
The juxtaposition of two or more components constitutes an assembly, and depending on the complexity of the arrangement, and on how far it may be thought to be self-evident from other information contained elsewhere in the set, it will need to be drawn at an appropriate scale for the benefit of the assembler. Figure **2.36**, taken from the UK Department of the Environment's PSA Library of Standard details, is an assembly drawing. Figure **2.37**, part of Foster Associates' highly sophisticated detailing for the Willis, Faber and Dumas head office building in Ipswich, is another. A world of technology lies between them, but each drawing has in common that it defines how a number of component parts are to be put together.

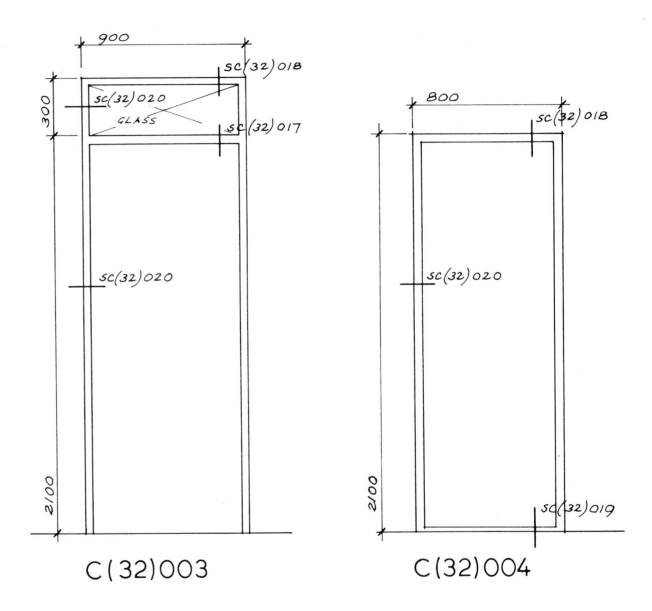

2.34 *Component drawing of different doorsets all cross-referenced back to standard sub-component drawing* (**2.35**)

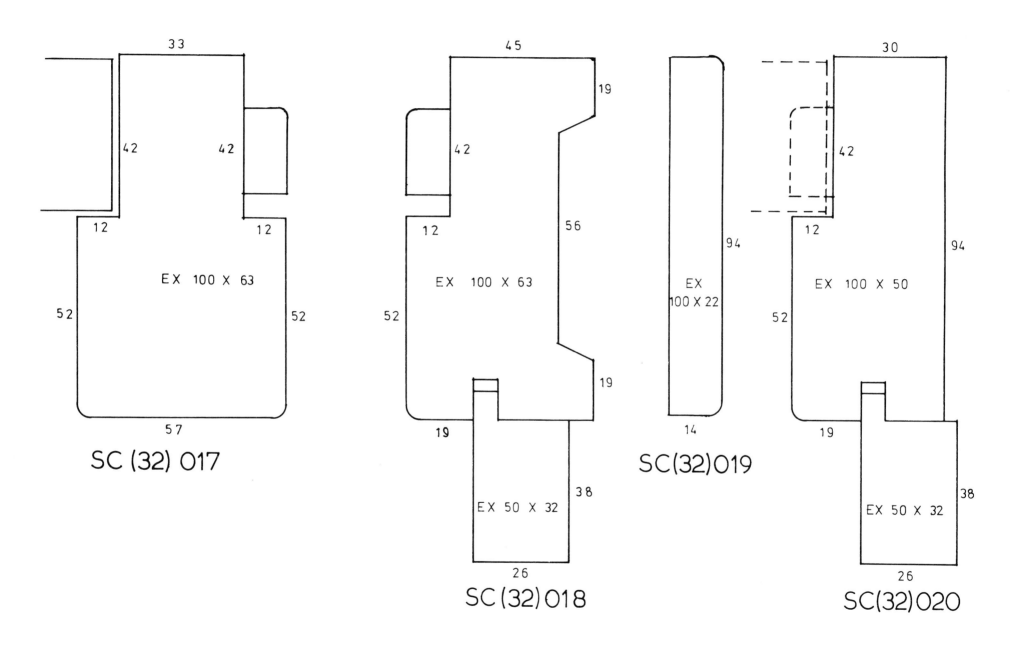

2.35 *Sub-component drawing illustrates constructional details of the component itself (scale full size)*

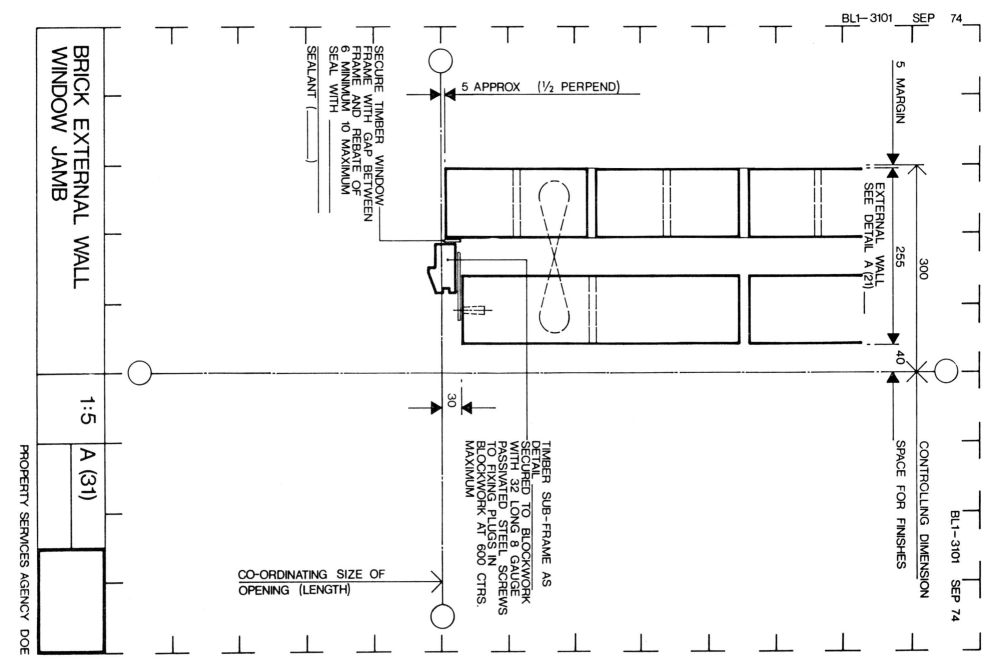

2.36 *Assembly detail from PSA Standard Library. Its simplicity contrasts sharply with the complexity of the detail illustrated in 2.37. What they have in common is that each conveys clearly and precisely the information needed by the operative carrying out the assembly*

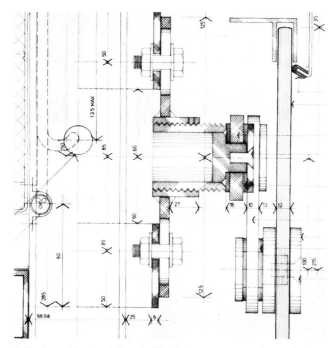

2.37 Assembly detail from Willis Faber and Dumas Head Office Building (Foster Associates)

With the assembly drawing we arrive at the very heart of the information package. If the location drawing is in many ways simply an ordered confirmation in building terms of planning decisions made long before, whilst the component drawing is frequently a documentation of the architect's judicious selection, the assembly drawing poses that most searching of all our questions, 'How is it to be built?'. Before he attempts to document his answer in a manner which is going to be acceptable to the users of the document, the detailer must not only be confident that he knows the answer, but also that he is aware of the full implications of the question.

It was stated at the outset that this book is not intended as a textbook on building construction, but it would be futile to pretend that the preparation of a set of working drawings can be regarded as an academic exercise, to be undertaken without reference to its content. Clearly form and content interact, and the point is raised now because it is precisely here, in the area of assembly detailing, that the really fundamental questions of adequacy emerge:
- Will the construction function adequately?
- Is the method of presentation adequate?
- Does the range of detailing anticipate adequately all the constructional problems that will be encountered by someone trying to erect the building?

Check lists are of limited value. There is really no substitute for the complete involvement of the detailer in his task, for an intelligent anticipation of the possible difficulties, for an alert awareness of the total problem while individual aspects of it are being dealt with. Nevertheless, it is useful at times to review one's work formally, if only because to do so concentrates the mind wonderfully. Since two distinct aspects of detailing are involved, two lists may be formulated.

The first, aimed at establishing the adequacy of the individual assembly detail, is a series of questions:
1. Is the chosen method of construction sound, particularly with regard to:
- possible movement
- water or damp penetration
- condensation
- cold bridging

2. Has it been adequately researched, particularly if non-traditional methods, or the use of proprietary products, are involved?
3. Is it reasonable to ask someone to construct it? Figure **2.38**—taken from a real but anonymous detail and calling for an improbably dexterous plasterer—is an example of the sort of thing that can occur when this question isn't asked.
4. What happens to the construction in plan (if the detail happens to be a sectional view) or in section (if the detail happens to show a plan view)?
5. Is the result going to be acceptable visually, both inside and outside?
6. Does the information concerned give rise to any possible ambiguity, or conflict with other information given elsewhere?

These questions are self-evident, and the conscientious draughtsman should have them in mind constantly from the outset of the detailing. They are noted here because it is probably better to pose them once more, formally, on completion of the series of details, than to have to worry about them at random in the small hours of the morning at some later date.

The second check list, aimed at determining the completeness of assembly detailing throughout the building, is more capable of precise definition. The objective is to cover the building comprehensively, identifying those aspects which merit the provision of assembly information about them. A logical progression is essential, and a suitable vehicle is readily to hand in CI/SfB table 1 (see p. 20) for not only does this provide an analysis of the building in elemental form but it also affords a framework within which the necessary details, once they are identified, may be presented.

It should be noted here that almost all the assembly detailing with which the architect will be concerned is confined to the primary and secondary elements, sections (2–) and (3–) of table 1. (The range of built-up fittings inherent in section (7–) should in general be regarded as components rather than assemblies.) Nevertheless, the exercise should be undertaken comprehensively.

The important things to note about assembly drawings are these:

1. *The scale must be appropriate to the complexity of the construction being detailed* In practice this will involve a scale of 1:20 being used for a wide variety of constructions, with a scale of 1:5 being used where greater detailed explanation is required—eg where the exact positioning of relatively small components such as bricks or tiles is a vital part of the information to be conveyed.

The level of draughting ability may well be a deciding factor here. But don't be over-optimistic, the mere fact

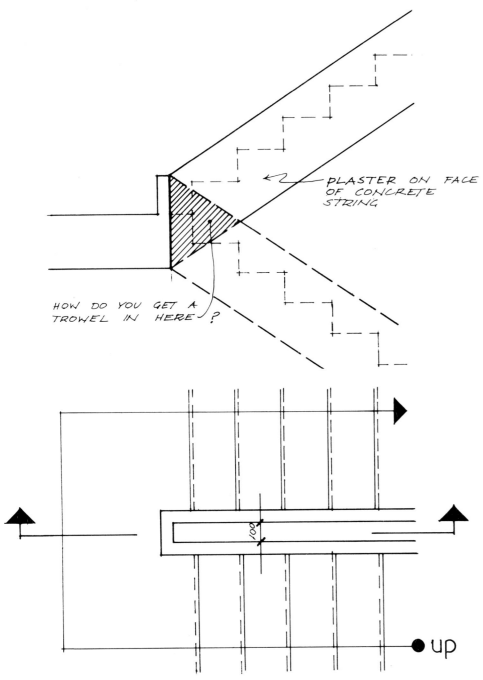

2.38 *Not an easy task for any plasterer*

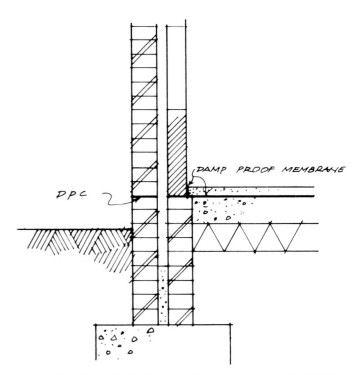

2.39 *Relatively simple detailing sensibly conveyed at a scale of 1:20*

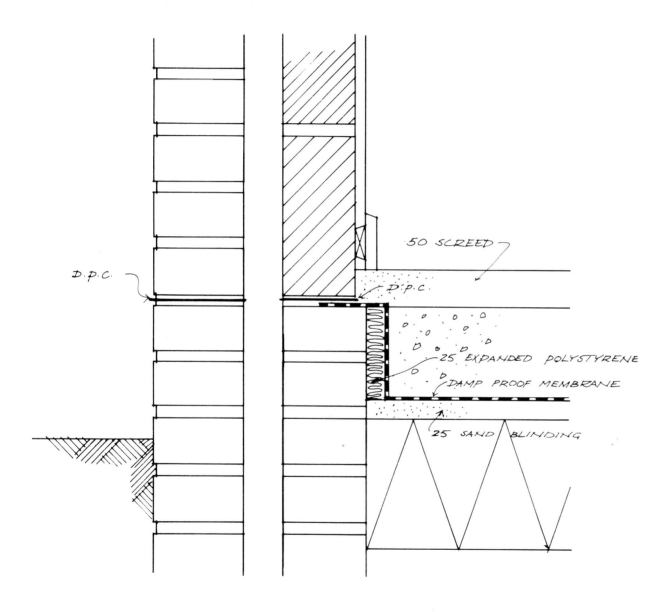

2.40 *Scale of 1:5 is necessary to show this detailing adequately*

of drawing to a larger scale will force you into consideration of problems which might have been glossed over at a smaller scale. It is the operative ultimately who will be asking the questions and requiring the drawn answer. And he will be building full size.

Figures **2.39** and **2.40** at scales of 1:20 and 1:5 respectively are appropriate examples of the information it is necessary to convey. Note that the damp course in **2.39**, being a simple layer of lead-cored bituminous felt, can be shown adequately at the smaller scale, whereas the damp course in **2.40** is a much more complex piece of work, with all sorts of hazards should it be installed incorrectly, and justifies its more expansive 1:5 treatment.

2. *The information given should be limited* Perhaps concentrated is the better word. For it is more helpful to produce twenty assembly sections, each covering a limited portion of the structure, than to attempt an elaborate constructional cross-section through the entire building purporting to give detailed information about almost everything.

Figure **2.41** reduced here from its original scale of 1:20 is a good example of how not to do it. All that has been achieved is a very large sheet of paper, consisting of an internal elevation at an inappropriately large scale surrounded by a margin of detailing which through necessity has been portrayed at a smaller scale than would have been desirable. The drawing has clearly taken a considerable time to produce. This in itself may well have led to some frustration on the part of the builder or the quantity surveyor, who needed urgently to know the damp course detailing in the bottom left-hand corner, but had to wait for the gutter flashings at the top right-hand corner to be finalised before the drawing could be issued to him.

At the end of the day we have been shown in some detail what happens to the construction along a more or less arbitrary knifecut through the building at one

WORKING DRAWINGS HANDBOOK

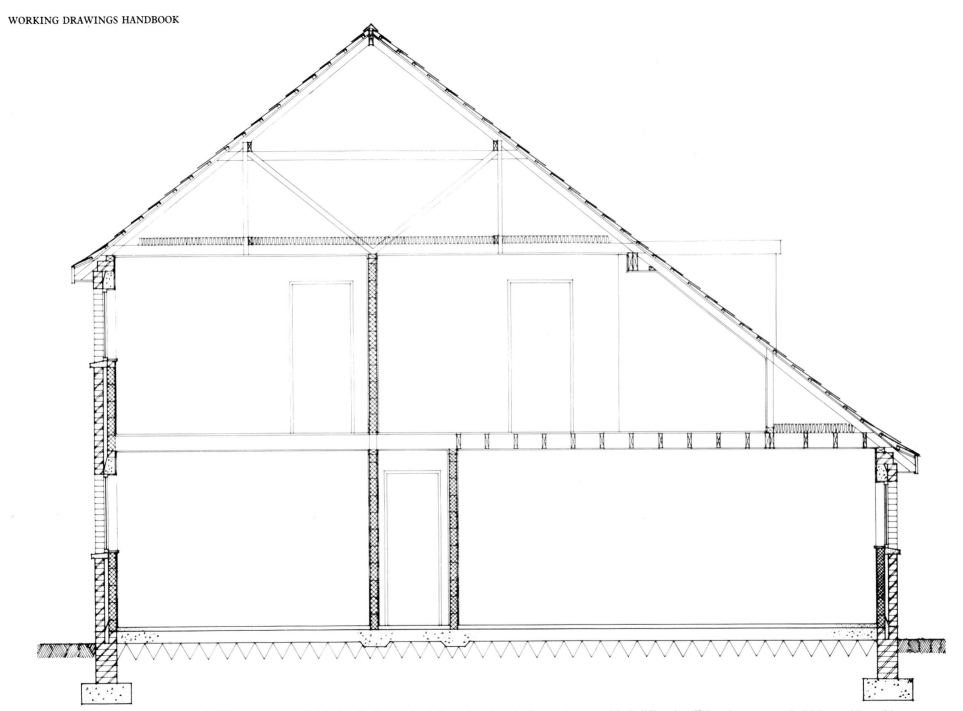

2.41 *Old-fashioned section through entire building. Far too detailed for its role of conveying information about the form and nature of the building; insufficient for anyone to build from with confidence*

point. It is to be hoped that the detailing is consistent right round the perimeter, because the detailer is not going to be anxious to repeat the exercise whenever the construction changes. Were he to do so he would find himself re-drawing 80 per cent of the information time and again in order that changes in the other 20 per cent could be properly recorded.

The more sensible way to deal with providing this sort of information is to prepare the assembly details in conjunction with, and related back to, the series of location sections described and advocated in the previous section on location drawings. The relevant information would then be cross-referenced on the lines of **2.42** and **2.43**.

3. *The assembly drawing should not be used to convey unnecessarily detailed information about the components from which it is to be produced* Consider the assembly section shown in **2.44**. The window frame is a standard section and will be bought in from a supplier ready for fixing into the structural opening. There was no need therefore to detail so lovingly and so explicitly the profiles of the frame and sub-frame, right down to the glazing beads and the throatings—they are matters of moment to the manufacturer in his workshop, not the erector on site. (The matter of prime importance to the erector, the method of fixing, is not mentioned at all—let us charitably assume that the point had been covered in the specification.) The only piece of information this assembly detail need convey about the window is its relationship to the surrounding components.

The detail might have been produced more simply and speedily as shown in **2.45**.

On the other hand it would be pedantic, especially on smaller projects, to reject the possibility offered by its large scale and availability of space round its margins, of providing descriptive annotation which it might be inconvenient to provide in another form. As elsewhere, comprehensiveness and common sense are the deciding factors.

4. *The information conveyed should be both comprehensive and, within the limits already defined for an assembly drawing, exhaustive* It should be comprehensive in the sense that the individual detail must contain all that the operative is going to need when he comes to that point on site. The detail may have been produced primarily to show the detailing of the window cill at a particular junction, but if it purports to show this junction then others will expect to use it for their own purposes, and it is no use being explicit about the window cill and vague about the wall finish beneath it. An assembly drawing is, by definition, a correlation of *all* the elements and trades involved.

So too the information should be exhaustive in the sense that no aspect of the construction, no variant on a basic detail, should be ambiguous or left to the discretion of the operative. 'Typical details' are just not good enough.

Coding assembly drawings
A complete system for coding the drawing package is discussed in chapter 4, but a note here on the coding of the drawings illustrated in **2.42** and **2.43** may be helpful.

The *location* section is coded: L for Location,
    (21) for external walls, 008 because it is the eighth detail in that particular series.
The *assembly* section is coded: A for Assembly,
    (31) for external openings, 003 because it is the third detail in its respective series.

The location section is coded (21)—not unreasonably, for its function is that it relates to the external walls. But then so does the assembly section. Why not code that (21) also?

The answer is that it would be perfectly in order to do so, and if you elected to produce a series of details devoted to the assembly problems encountered in constructing the external walls, then you would code them A (21) 001, etc accordingly. But it is more likely that in commencing a series of details showing the *junctions* of two elements—for example, the junction of external openings components with the external walls within which they sit—you would find it more convenient, and a better guarantee that you had covered the subject comprehensively, to produce a series of *external openings assembly details*—and these would naturally fall into the (31) series.

The examples of assembly details illustrated have consisted of vertical sections through a particular construction, but of course the plan section also requires illustration and enlargement at certain key points—doors and window jambs, for example.

Where this is the case, and where space allows, it is better to group plans and sections together by their common element rather than to produce a series of plan details on one sheet and a series of section details on another. Everyone on site concerned with forming the window opening, and with fixing the window into it, will then have the relevant information readily to hand.

The schedule
There are two distinct types of schedule.

There is the straightforward list of items, complete in itself, which adds little or nothing to information about its contents which may be obtained elsewhere in the drawings or in the specification. What it does is present this information in a more disciplined and readily retrievable form. A list of lighting fittings, collected on a room-by-room basis, is an example, providing a convenient document for the electrical contractor who has to order the fittings and a useful check list with which the architect can re-assure himself that none has been overlooked.

Schedules of manholes, of sanitary fittings, and of ironmongery are other instances of this type, as indeed is the drawing schedule.

Such schedules, carrying descriptive rather than graphical information, are better typed than drawn, and

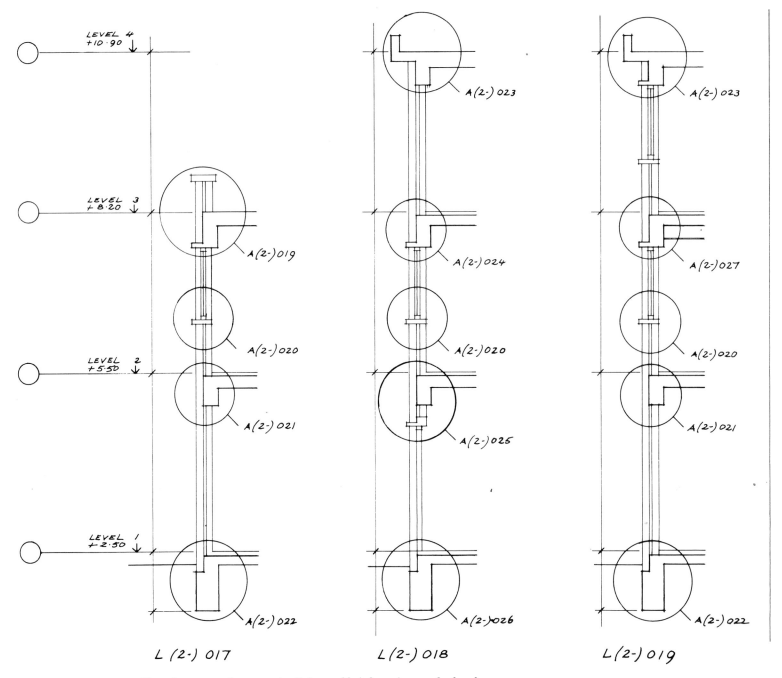

2.42 *Location section provides references to where more detailed assembly information may be found*

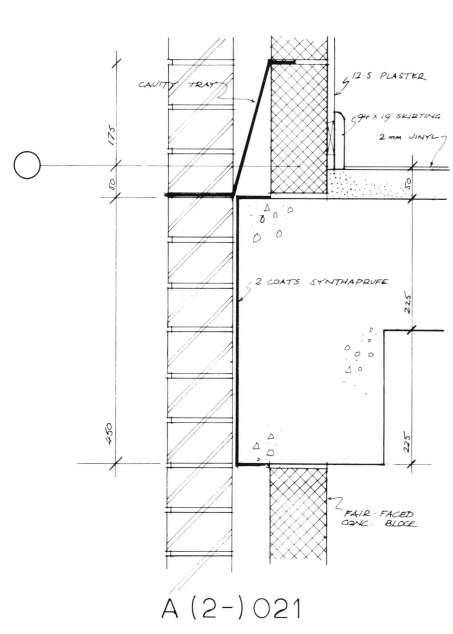

2.43 Assembly sections derived from 2.42

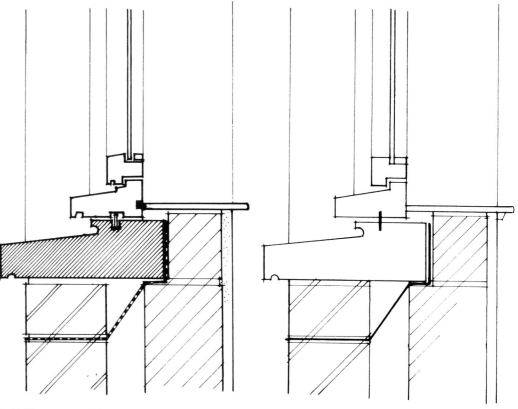

2.44 *Unnecessary elaboration wastes time and helps nobody*

2.45 *Simplified version of 2.44 gives adequate information to all concerned*

their natural home is more likely to be within the covers of the specification or bills of quantities than with the drawing set.

The other type of schedule is also component-oriented, but in addition to being a list it provides an essential link in the search pattern information by giving pointers as to where other information is to be found. Such schedules are of the type envisaged in (**1.9**) and commented upon in chapter 1. A useful format is shown in **2.46**.

Note that what is shown is neither a door schedule nor a window schedule, but an 'openings schedule'. It is important to maintain this concept if the drawing set is being structured using CI/SfB, because CI/SfB acknowledges only 'openings in external walls', 'openings in internal walls', 'openings in floors', and 'openings in roofs'. All components filling such openings require to be treated as part of the opening and hence are scheduled accordingly.

Even if use is made of some other elemental method of coding, however, it is still of advantage to follow the same pattern, for it enables information to be included in the schedule both about openings which are filled by no component—an arched opening, for example, or an unsealed serving hatch—and about openings filled by components which are neither doors nor windows—ventilator grilles, for example.

A form of schedule best avoided is what might be termed the 'vocabulary schedule'. An example is shown in **2.47**. The basis of this type of schedule is the vertical tabulation of the list of components or rooms, and the horizontal tabulation of an exhaustive list of ancillaries. The disadvantages of this method are two-fold. It is not always easy to be exhaustive in assessing at the outset the range of possible ancillaries, with the result that the subsequent introduction of another item disrupts the tabulation. And the use of dots or crosses to indicate which ancillary is required is visually confusing and prone to error.

OPENING				COMPONENT		ASSEMBLY DRAWINGS REFERRING			
OPENING NO	ROOM NAME/NO	CO-ORDINATING DIMS		TYPE/ DRG. NO	DESCRIPTION	JAMB (VIEWED FROM INSIDE ROOM)		HEAD	CILL
		HEIGHT	WIDTH			L.H.	R.H.		
(32) G 001	G/2	2100	900	C(3-)001	DOOR	A(3-)002	A(3-)002	A(3-)002	—
(32) G 002	G/1	2100	900	C(3-)001	"	A(3-)002	A(3-)002	A(3-)002	—
(32) G 003	G/2	2100	900	C(3-)001	"	A(3-)002	A(3-)002	A(3-)002	—
(32) G 004	G/6	2100	800	C(3-)002	"	A(3-)003	A(3-)003	A(3-)001	—
(32) G 005	G/6	2100	800	C(3-)002	"	A(3-)001	A(3-)001	A(3-)001	—
(32) G 006	G/7	2100	800	C(3-)002	"	A(3-)003	A(3-)003	A(3-)001	—
(32) G 007	G/7	2100	800	C(3-)002	"	A(3-)001	A(3-)001	A(3-)001	—
(32) G 008	G/5	AS MANUFACTURER'S CAT.		MAGNET MCF 26	"	—	—	—	—
(32) G 009	G/4	"	"	MAGNET MCF 36	"	—	—	—	—
(32) G 010	G/2	1100	300	C(38)002	VISION PANEL	A(38)002	A(38)002	A(38)002	A(38)002
(32) G 011	G/1	SHOP FITTERS' SUPPLY		—	WICKET GATE	—	—	—	—

2.46 *Useful format for an openings schedule*

TYPES OF DRAWING

Door No	1 pair of lever handles	2 back plate with ① L.H.	3 back plate with ① R.H.	4 pair of knobs 47 mm	5 back plate with ④ L.H.	6 back plate with ④ R.H.	7 Taylor's spindle	8 push plate 150 × 75	9 push plate 225 × 75	10 escutcheon (for locks)	11 escutcheon (for latch)	12 single pull handle 150mm	13 single pull handle 225mm	14 door stop – floor	15 door stop – wall	16 indicator bolt	17 flush bolt – 225 mm	18 barrel bolt – 100 mm	19 mortise panic bolt	20 cylinder lock	21 overhead door closer	22 H.D. ditto	23 floor spring – single	24 floor spring – double	25 upright mortise lock for ①	26 upright mortise lock for ④	27 upright mortise latch	28 kicking plate – 150 mm	29 kicking plate – 225 mm
G/11								●				●											●						●
G/12								●				●											●						●
G/13	●	●								●				●													●		
G/14	●	●								●					●						●						●		
G/15	●		●							●					●												●		
G/16	●		●							●				●							●						●		
1/01				●		●	●		●								●								●				
1/02	●	●																									●		
1/03	●	●																									●		
1/04	●		●																								●		
1/05									●			●			●						●								
1/06	●	●																									●		
1/07	●	●																									●		
1/08								●				●				●					●								
1/09	●	●																									●		
1/10				●	●		●			●																●			
1/11	●	●								●							●						●						
1/12	●		●								●																	●	
1/13	●		●							●						●										●			

2.47 'Vocabulary' type of schedule. It is dangerously easy to get a dot in the wrong place

SET NO	ITEM	MAKE	CAT. REF.
1	pair of lever handles pair of back plates pair of insert escutcheons	Modric " "	A 3001 A 6001 A 2104
2	pair of knobs (47 mm) pair of back plates	" "	A 2501 A 600
3	pair of lever handles pair of back plates pair of insert escutcheons overhead door closer	" " " "	A 3001 A 6001 A 2104 A 9106
4	push plate single pull handle indicator bolt overhead door closer	" " " "	A 6800 A 1202 A 5001 A 9106

2.48 *Lists of ironmongery collected into sets*

A more rational way of dealing with this ironmongery schedule would be to collect the individual items of ironmongery into series of sets, and to indicate which set is required against the individual door or window component in the openings schedule illustrated in **2.46**. The listing of ironmongery sets would then be as shown in **2.48**, and the addition to the schedule would appear as in **2.49**.

Pictorial views
The use of perspective sketches, axonometrics and exploded views should not be overlooked as a means of conveying assembly information which might be difficult to document in more conventional forms. Nor should the value of pictorial elevations, perspectives, photo montages and models be discounted as an aid to the contractor. Photographs of existing buildings are invaluable to an estimator when pricing demolition or rehabilitation work, and a model, or a photograph of one, will often demonstrate site management problems to the contractor's planning team more succinctly than a collection of plans and sections.

Such pictorial aids should be clearly defined as being for informational purposes only, and not possessing contractual significance.

Specification
The function of the specification in relation to a competent and comprehensive set of drawings may be defined quite simply. It is to set out quality standards for materials and workmanship in respect of building elements whose geometry, location and relationships one to another have been described by means of the drawings.

It follows, therefore, that in a properly structured information package neither specification nor drawings should trespass upon the other's territory. If the drawing calls for roofing felt then it need describe it simply as that—'roofing felt', or 'built-up felt roofing'. If only one type of built-up roofing felt construction is to be used on the project then that simple description suffices. If more than one, then 'built-up felt roofing type I' will be a sufficient indication of intent. To the specification will then fall the task of describing in detail just what 'built-up felt roofing type I' is to consist of.

Conversely, the specification is no place for instructions such as 'Cover the roof of the boiler house in three layers of built-up felt roofing'. If a specific roof surface is to be so covered, then it is the function of the drawings to tell everybody so, when the full extent of the covering and the possible operational problems in achieving it may be clearly and simply described.

This simple differentiation between the roles of drawings and specification will enable each to fulfil its true function properly.

OPENING				COMPONENT		ASSEMBLY DRAWINGS REFERRING				ANCILLARIES		
OPENING NO	ROOM NAME/NO	CO-ORDINATING DIMS		TYPE/ DRG. NO	DESCRIPTION	JAMB (VIEWED FROM INSIDE ROOM)		HEAD	CILL	LINTOL TYPE / DRG. NO.	IRON- MONGERY SET NO.	LOCK REF.
		HEIGHT	WIDTH			L.H.	R.H.					
(32) 001	9/2	2100	900	C(3-)001	DOOR	A(3-)002	A(3-)002	A(3-)002	—	TYPE A	3	AB304
(32) 002	9/1	2100	900	C(3-)001	"	A(3-)002	A(3-)002	A(3-)002	—	TYPE A	2	AB301
(32) 003	9/2	2100	900	C(3-)001	"	A(3-)002	A(3-)002	A(3-)002	—	TYPE B	2	AB301
(32) 004	9/6	2100	800	C(3-)002	"	A(3-)003	A(3-)003	A(3-)001	—	NONE	4	—
(32) 005	9/6	2100	800	C(3-)002	"	A(3-)001	A(3-)001	A(3-)001	—	NONE	4	—
(32) 006	9/7	2100	800	C(3-)002	"	A(3-)003	A(3-)003	A(3-)001	—	NONE	4	—
(32) 007	9/7	2100	800	C(3-)002	"	A(3-)001	A(3-)001	A(3-)001	—	NONE	4	—

2.49 *The openings schedule shown in* **2.46** *extended to give information about ironmongery sets*

3 Draughtsmanship

Drawing reproduction
All drawings dealt with in this book will need to be drawn in a form from which copies can be taken. It is self-evident that the copies should be clearly legible, durable enough for their intended purpose and inexpensive to produce.

For all practical purposes day-to-day reproduction of drawings is confined to two processes.

Electro-static copying
The image is formed on a photo-conductive surface, this surface being either an integral part of the copy paper, or applied to a revolving drum which in turn prints the image on to plain paper fed into it.

The process has the advantage that the original may be on opaque paper, but in its present state of development it suffers from limitations of paper size. Most machines have a maximum size of A4, and even the two or three expensive copiers at the upper end of the market fail to go beyond A3.

Diazo or dyeline copying
The alternative process relies upon ultra-violet light passing through a translucent original and activating diazonium salts carried on the copy paper. The image thus formed is developed by the action of ammonia vapour or a liquid developer. Most machines in this field will take paper up to 1200 mm wide and (if supplied in roll form) of virtually unlimited length.

Since the ability to copy large drawings is of paramount importance almost all working drawings will need to be drawn on a traslucent medium of some kind. Indeed, even A4 drawings, which might in theory be drawn satisfactorily on opaque paper for electro-static reproduction, will often in practice be built up by a combination of original drawing and tracing from other drawings or sketches, rendering the use of a transparent sheet highly desirable.

For all practical purposes, therefore, the following comments about drawing techniques may be taken as applying to one or other of the three transparent media available.

Materials
Detail paper
This has the great advantage of being cheap and, because it offers a semi-opaque background, pleasant and satisfying to draw on, particularly in pencil. Against this must be set the fact that it is not an ideal medium for dyeline reproduction, giving insufficient contrast when compared with other media. If a lighter grade is used to improve its translucency (weights vary between 50 and 70 g/m^2), then it becomes vulnerable to tearing and over-enthusiastic erasure.

Detail paper has its uses, but these are best limited to the preparation of drafts for subsequent tracing into final drawings, where the original sheet may be expected to have a limited life and where any prints taken from it will be for internal exchange of information among team members, and to rapidly-produced short-life pencil details (accompanying architect's instructions, for example).

It should not be used for drawings forming part of the original production set.

Tracing paper
This, by far the most common medium to be found in drawing office use today, is available in a wide range of weights (from 50 to 112 g/m^2) and surface textures (smooth, semi-matt and matt).

A smooth finish is desirable, especially for pencil work, where the more abrasive surfaces of the matt and semi-matt finishes tend to wear down pencil points rapidly, and are more difficult to keep clean during preparation of the drawing.

A weight of 90 g/m^2 is probably the most common in general use in drawing offices, but it is arguable that 112 g/m² paper justifies its extra cost. It is dimensionally more stable and less liable to go brittle with age. (Liability to buckling and dimensional instability through variations in humidity are two characteristics of all tracing papers.) It stands up better to heavy-handed erasing and it is less liable to damage than the lighter papers, a particularly important consideration in a large project which is going to be around for some years.

Drafting film
This has virtually superseded tracing cloth as a high quality product when durability is a prime requirement. It has other advantages which make it a contender, despite its high cost. It is dimensionally stable; it takes ink and pencil well; both may be erased easily. However, it is very hard on the normal technical pen, and it is desirable to use a range with specially hardened tips.

A major disadvantage in practical use is the fact that ink dries slowly, the film being totally non-absorbent and reliant upon evaporation alone for drying.

All in all, a good quality tracing paper offers the most practical all-round medium for general use.

Ink or pencil
Of the two available media for drawing lines the choice rests, to some extent, with the personal inclinations and particular abilities of the draughtsman. Many find pencil the more sympathetic medium, with its wide range of line inflexions, and a pencil drawing is normally a more personal document, reflective of the draughtsman's character, than the ink equivalent. The function of a working drawing, however, is the unambiguous conveyance of drawn information, and aesthetic considerations must remain secondary.

The relative advantages and disadvantages of both media are listed below, but on the whole considerations of permanence and reprographic clarity make ink the more suitable for the bulk of the final production set of drawings.

This is not to rule out the use of pencil altogether. Its speed, particularly when applied with self-confidence, makes it suitable for the production of large-scale details, full sizes of joinery sections, etc and supplementary details urgently needed on site. It is also useful as an adjunct to what are otherwise pen and ink drawings—for the addition of hatching, for example, which can be a time-consuming process in ink.

Ink—advantages
- Consistent density of line
- Reprographic clarity
- Permanence of image
- Completeness of erasure (by razor blade or mechanical eraser).

Ink—disadvantages
- Relatively slow process
- Set-square and scales liable to smudge still wet lines
- Erasure somewhat laborious.

Pencil—advantages
- Speed of execution
- Wide range of line character
- Rapid erasure of errors and changes.

Pencil—disadvantages
- Liability to smudging of completed lines
- Necessity for constant re-sharpening of pencil
- Difficulty of keeping sheet clean during preparation
- Difficulty of complete erasure.

Techniques
Line thickness
Ink techniques: The old-fashioned adjustable ruling pen offered an infinite gradation of line thickness. Now that it has been superseded, for all practical purposes, by various systems of pens with interchangeable points of differing pre-determined thickness, the draughtsman is faced with the question of selecting from a very wide range of line thickness a limited number that may be used to give the appropriate degree of emphasis to different aspects of his drawing. It is clearly desirable to establish a convention whereby definable aspects of a drawing are always delineated at a given thickness, and in doing this it is likely that the line thickness requirements of such aspects will vary with the size, scale and function of the drawing.

Among the manufacturers of technical pens, there are two ranges of point thickness in common use. The earlier, and at the moment understandably the better established, offers the following line thicknesses:
Range 1 (thickness of line in mm): 0.1, 0.15, 0.2, 0.3, 0.4, 0.5, 0.6, 0.8, 1.0, 1.2.
The alternative is based on German DIN Standards and offers the following:
Range 2 (thickness of line in mm): 0.13, 0.18, 0.25, 0.35, 0.5, 0.7, 1.0, 1.4, 2.0.
Both ranges are shown at full size in **3.1**.

Range 2 offers greater flexibility at the lower end of the scale, and the claim is made for it that it is better adapted for photographic enlargement or reduction of originals (when this is confined to the 'A' range of sheet sizes). It will be seen that each size in the range doubles the thickness alternately preceding it, with the result that alterations may be carried out to an enlarged or reduced copy negative in a similar weight of line to that appearing on the copy. (A similar facility is available in the Range 1 thicknesses by judicious selection.)

It must be said that the likelihood of this facility being utilised in normal working drawing practice is fairly remote. Advanced techniques are discussed in chapter 5, however, where the 1:2 reduction of negatives is an essential feature of the method (see 'Overlay draughting'). For 1:2 reduction of negatives the minimum recommended line thickness for use on the original drawing is 0.25 mm, allowing the use of the minimum size 0.13 pen for any alterations. In fact the general principle holds good, that in any process of reduction the minimum line thickness on the final print should not be less than 0.13 mm if legibility and uniformity of reproduction are to be maintained.

But for the normal production of working drawing negatives, where reproduction may be expected to be a 1:1 ratio, there is no reason why a thickness of 0.18 or 0.2 should not be selected for the thinnest line used.

Three different line thicknesses will suffice for most drawings. If we term them *a*, *b* and *c,* with *a* being the thinnest and *c* the thickest, the various parts of a drawing may be grouped within them as follows:

range one

Line thickness in mm

0.1

0.15

0.2

0.3

0.4

0.5

0.6

0.8

1.2

range two

Line thickness in mm

0.13

0.18

0.25

0.35

0.5

0.7

1.0

1.4

2.0

3.1 *The range of line thicknesses available with the use of technical pens*

a grid line
  centre lines
  dimension lines
  leader lines
  incidental furniture, etc where relevant
  hatching
b all other lines, with the exception of:
c those lines, particularly on an elementalised drawing, which it is desired to emphasise, either because they define the element which is the subject of the drawing, or in the general interest of clarity.

The values to be set against the three categories will vary with the scale and nature of the drawings, and with the range of pen sizes selected. Table III provides adequate differentiation of line while at the same time limiting the necessary range of equipment to five pen sizes:

Table III Recommended pen sizes

	a	b	c		
1 Drawings to a scale of 1:50 and less	a	b	c		
2 Drawings to a scale of 1:20 to 1:5		a	b	c	
3 Drawings to a scale larger than 1:5			a	b	c
Pen size Range 1	0.2	0.3	0.4	0.5	0.7
Pen size Range 2	0.18	0.25	0.35	0.5	0.7

Figures **3.2** and **3.3**, taken from parts of drawings of various scales, have been redrawn using both pen size ranges for comparison.

Pencil techniques: The preceding comments on differentiation between line thickness also hold good in principle when the medium employed is pencil on tracing paper.

Here, however, we are concerned with a medium which can vary the density of a line as well as its thickness, and both techniques are used to define the importance of a given line. Generally speaking, both density and thickness are functions of the grade of pencil or lead employed, and of the pressure used.

4H and 2H will normally suffice, but the implications of drawing for dyeline reproduction are greater for pencil than for ink. Reasonably firm pressure is needed on the pencil to ensure that a full and dense line is produced, and when this is applied injudiciously, indentations can be left in the paper after subsequent erasure. These indentations may remain as ghost lines on the print.

Drawing sheet size
The international 'A' series of paper sizes is now universally accepted and all drawings and printed sheets likely to be used in the office will conform to its requirements. It originates in the ingenious concept of a rectangle having an area of 1m², the length of whose sides are in the proportions $1:\sqrt{2}$ (**3.4**).

The dimensions of this rectangle will be found to be 1189 × 841 mm, and by progressively halving the larger dimension each time, a reducing series of rectangles is produced, in which the proportions of the original rectangle remain unchanged and in which the area of each rectangle is half that of its predecessor in the series (**3.5**).

The range of 'A' sizes available to the drawing office is as follows:

A0 1189 × 841 mm	A3 420 × 297 mm
A1 841 × 594 mm	A4 297 × 210 mm
A2 594 × 420 mm	

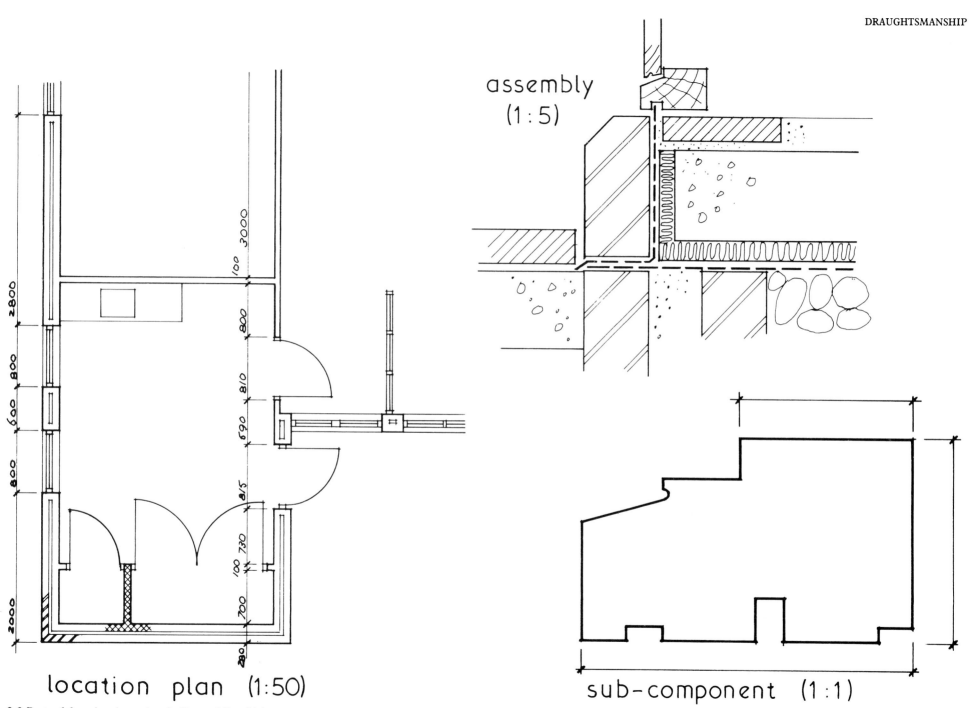

3.2 *Parts of three drawings using the Range 1 line thicknesses*

WORKING DRAWINGS HANDBOOK

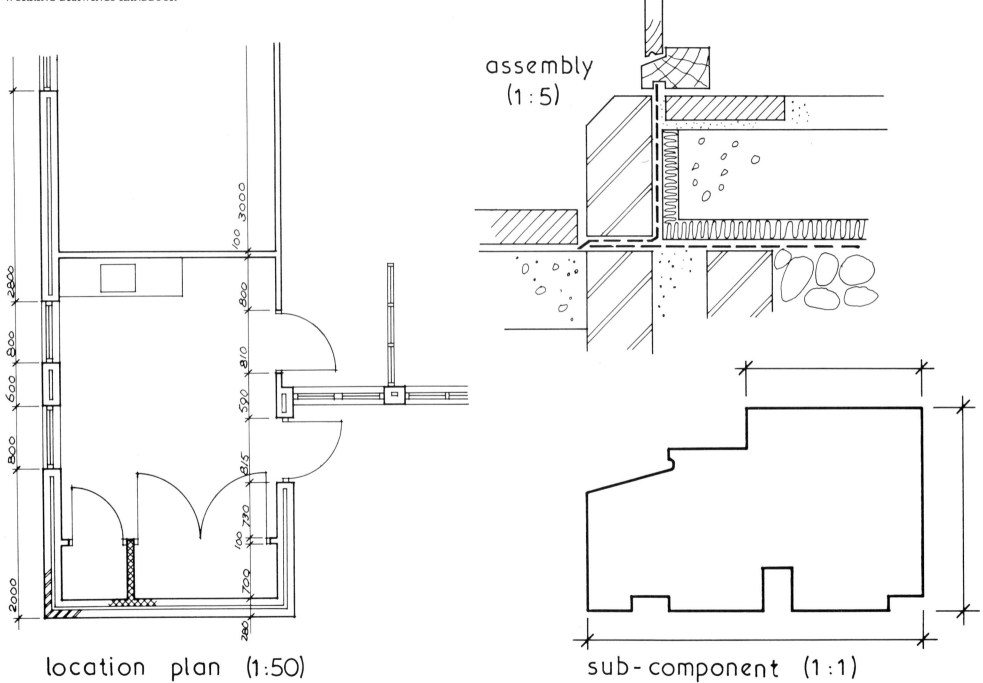

3.3 *The drawings shown in* **3.2** *re-drawn using the recommended Range 2 line thicknesses*

The large differential between A0 and A1 has led to the introduction in some offices of a bastard sized sheet to reduce the gap, but the use of intermediate sizes is not desirable. They have to be cut from paper of a larger standard size, and their non-standard proportions lead to difficulties in both storage and photographic reduction.

Indeed, both these and the A0 sheet should be avoided wherever possible. The A0 sheet is incredibly cumbersome both in the drawing office and on site, and on the whole it would seem to be preferable to set the A1 sheet as an upper limit in all but the most exceptional circumstances. The site plan for even the largest of projects can always be illustrated at the appropriate scale on a number of marginally overlapping smaller sheets, with, if necessary, a key sheet drawn more simply at a smaller scale to show the whole extent of the site (**3.6**).

Where an area is sub-divided in this fashion a small key plan should always form part of the title block to indicate the relationship of that particular drawing to the overall plan (**3.7**).

Apart from this upper limitation it is clearly sensible to restrict as far as possible the number of different sized drawings issued on any one project. An early appraisal of the size of the job and of the appropriate scale for the location plans will probably establish the format for the complete set of location drawings, and normally it is not difficult to contrive that the assemblies and the ranges of component drawings should also be drawn on sheets of that size.

The majority of the drawings in the average set therefore will appear in either A1 or A2 format, depending upon the size of the project.

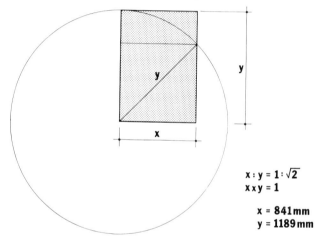

$x : y = 1 : \sqrt{2}$
$x \times y = 1$

$x = 841\,\text{mm}$
$y = 1189\,\text{mm}$

3.4 *Derivation of the rectangle A0 with a surface area of 1 square metre*

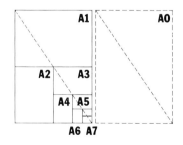

3.5 *'A' sizes retain the same proportions ($1:\sqrt{2}$). Each sheet is half the size of its predecessor*

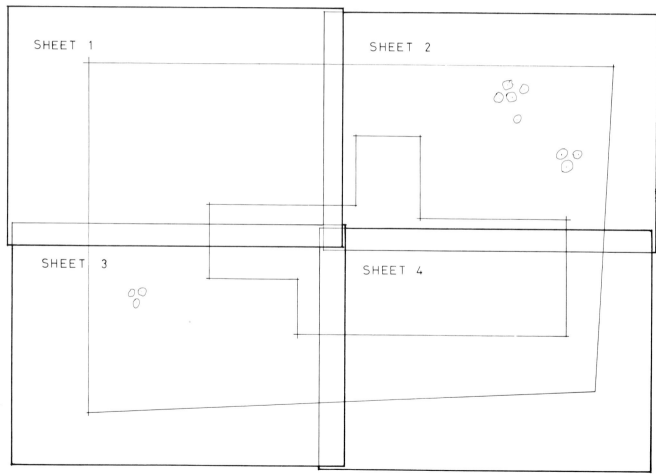

3.6 *Overlapping smaller sheets allow the appropriate scale to be used for the plan of a large area without recourse to unwieldy A0 sheets*

The nature of sub-component drawings and schedules, however, tends to make a smaller format more suitable for them, and there will always be in addition a number of isolated small details on any project which it would be pointless to draw in one corner of an A1 sheet, and which it would be confusing to attempt to collect together on a single sheet (the 'miscellaneous details' approach which has been condemned earlier).

Where the format for the other drawings is A2 it is probably worth wasting a little paper for the sake of obtaining a manageable set of consistent size. Where the general size is A1, however, a smaller sheet becomes necessary, and whether this should be A4 or A3 is a matter for some debate.

A3 or A4? It may be helpful to set out the pros and cons. The advantages of the A4 format are:

- A substantial amount of the project information is already in A4 format—specification, bills of quantities, architect's instructions, correspondence, etc
- Trade literature is normally A4, and if you wish to include manufacturers' catalogues as part of your set (and why not?), then they are more readily absorbed into the structure of the set if you already have an A4 category
- Most users—both producer and recipient—will possess or have access to an A4 photo-copier with the facility that this offers to, for example, the contractor who wishes to get alternative quotes for a particular item and can rapidly produce his own copies of the particular drawing. The A3 copier is still something of an expensive rarity
- The restricted size of sheet makes it more suitable for producing standard drawings, where it is necessary to limit the amount and extent of the information shown in order to preserve its 'neutrality'
- Architect's instructions are frequently accompanied by a sketch detail and the A4 format simplifies filing and retrieval
- A bound set of A4 drawings is suitable for shelf storage. A3s are an inconvenient size to store, whether on a shelf, in a plan chest drawer, or in a vertifile
- A4s can be carried around easily.

The disadvantages of the A4 format are:

- The drawing area is altogether too small. One is constantly being forced into the position of limiting what is shown because there just is not room on the paper, or of selecting an inappropriately small scale
- There is no room to record amendments adequately, nor for that matter to incorporate a reasonably informative title panel
- Builders don't like them.

The choice is not easy, but on the whole the author is inclined to favour A3 as the smallest sheet of a set, if only for the pragmatic reasons that you can, at a pinch, hang them landscape in a vertifile; that you can, at a pinch, bind them into a specification or a bill of quantities and fold them double; that you can, at a pinch, copy them in two halves on an electro-static copier and sellotape the two halves together; and that wasting paper is, in the last resort, cheaper than re-drawing a detail which in the end just would not quite go on the sheet.

Drawing conventions
Building elements
In the same way that line thickness is influenced by considerations of scale and the relative importance of the objects delineated, so too is the degree of detail by which various elements are represented. The manner in which a door or a window is shown on a 1:20 assembly drawing is not necessarily appropriate to their representation on a 1:200 location plan.

As always, common sense and absolute clarity of expression are the criteria. If a door frame is detailed elsewhere in the set at a scale large enough for the intricacies of its mouldings to be described accurately, then it is a waste of time and a possible source of confusion if an attempt is made to reproduce the mouldings on a 1:20 assembly drawing whose real function is to indicate the frame's position in relation to the wall in which it sits.

Some conventional methods of representation which are generally speaking appropriate for a range of elements at various scales are given in appendix 1.

Handing and opening
The conventions for describing the side on which a door

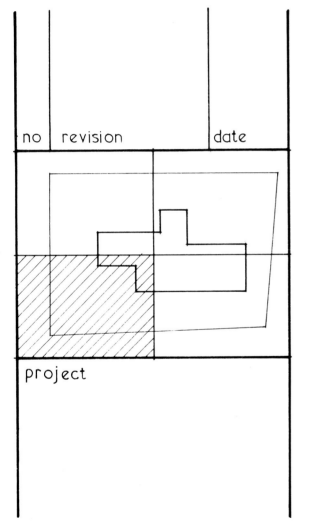

3.7 *Key to sub-divided plan forms part of the title block*

is hung are many and varied. These are sometimes ambiguous, at worst contradictory, and few areas where precise description is vital suffer so much in practice from imprecision as this one.

Possibly the simplest and most easily remembered convention is this: that the hand of an opening is the side on which the hinges may be seen.

The use of this convention provides a ready mental reference for checking the handing of any component, and for providing instructions to others. Like any other convention, however, it is of little use to the recipient unless he is in on the secret. So he must be told, preferably by a simple statement at the start of the component schedules.

The conventions determining window openings are in more general use, presumably through the early development of the metal window industry with its requirements for off-site hanging of casements and a consequent clear system for describing the handing.

The normally accepted convention is that the window is drawn as viewed from the outside. Conventional representations for both door and window openings are given in appendix 2.

Hatching

The use of hatching of various kinds to give a graphical indication of different materials was first developed as a readily reproducible alternative to the laborious colouring of opaque originals which had preceded it. BS 1192:1969 set out a range of conventions for various materials, and PD 6479:1976 has subsequently proposed co-ordination into a definitive recommendation of existing conventions currently in use within various disciplines.

The existing ranges of conventions are all based on building techniques of the last century, and were they to be brought fully up to date an enormous expansion of conventions would be necessary. Such concepts as rigid and loose-fill insulation, for example, fibre-glass mouldings, or glass-reinforced cement would all require consideration.

One should first question the necessity, or indeed the desirability, of hatching in the first place. BS 1192 itself suggests that it only be used when confusion is likely to occur in the interpretation of drawings, and in most cases such potential confusion may usually be avoided by other means. Building elements shown in section, for example, may be distinguished from lines in elevation or grid lines by affording each their proper line thickness, without recourse to hatching. Different materials are less likely to be confused with one another when drawings are elementalised; and in any case the mere differentiation between, say, brickwork and blockwork which is possible with hatching is not normally sufficiently precise for present day purposes. We want to know if the bricks are commons, or engineering quality, or facings. We want to know if the blockwork is lightweight for insulating purposes or dense and load-bearing. Such subtleties can only be covered by proper annotation, and such annotation will often render other methods redundant.

Where hatching is used (and BS 1192 itself suggests that this be limited to larger-scale drawings), it should be kept simple in convention. Often a simple diagonal hatching, with the diagonals running in different directions, will suffice to illustrate the function of two components of the same material, without requiring that the user look up some vast code book to see what the material is. He is told that in the accompanying notes.

Gridded hatching, where the grid is parallel to the axes of the element being hatched, is not only time-consuming to draw but downright confusing to interpret.

Some conventions in common use, simplified from their original sources in some instances, are given in appendix 3, but their use should be very much conditioned by the comments above.

Electrical symbols

The architect frequently becomes involved in the production of electrical layout drawings, particularly on smaller projects where no M & E consultant is engaged, and appendix 4 gives some of the more commonly used symbols in general practice.

Two points may usefully be made about the method of showing wiring links between switch and fitting. In the first place, of course, any such representation on the drawing is purely diagrammatic; no attempt need be made to indicate the precise route the wiring should take. (If ducted provision has been made the fact should be noted on the drawing, and the ducting shown on the appropriate builder's work drawing.)

In the second place, the links are far better drawn free-hand than in straight lines which are liable to conflict with other building elements (see **2.8**).

Non-active lines

Lines on a drawing which delineate the actual building fabric are termed 'active lines'. Those lines which are essential to our understanding of the drawing, but which form no part of the building, such as grid lines, dimension lines, direction arrows, etc are termed 'non-active lines'.

Recommended conventions for non-active lines are given in appendix 5.

Templates

Numerous plastic cut-out templates are now on the market covering many of the symbols given in the appendixes. Templates are also available for the production of circles and ellipses, and for drawing sanitary fittings.

Such templates are a time-saving aid, even though one of the corollaries of Murphy's Law ensures that the symbol you really need is missing from that particular template. A word of warning should be added about the indiscriminate use of templates for sanitary fittings,

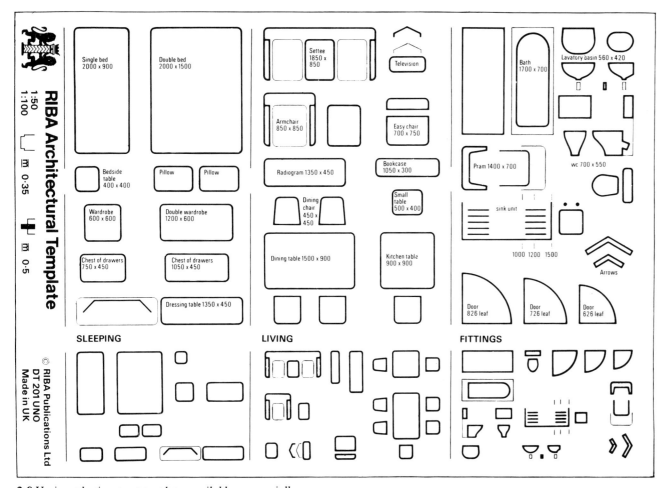 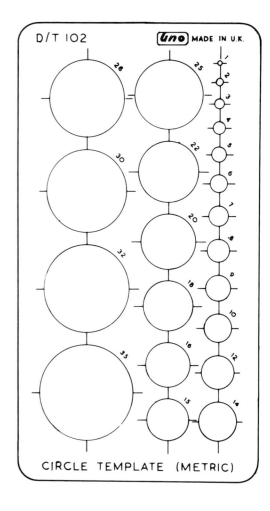

3.8 *Various plastic cut-out templates available commercially*

where it is dangerously easy to fool yourself about dimensions. Some manufacturers of sanitary fittings produce their own templates and these, of course, give an accurate representation of the particular fitting specified, but in their absence it is safer to draw the fitting to its true overall dimensions taken from the manufacturer's catalogue than to rely on a standard template which may deceive you into a situation where the toilet door fouls the lavatory basin which arrived on site larger than you had drawn it.

Sheets of stick-on and dry transfer symbols are also obtainable and offer a reasonable choice. They are dangerous, however, in that the symbols are liable to rub off with constant use of the negative, with potentially disastrous consequences.

Figure **3.8** shows a range of templates.

Dimensioning
This is a somewhat more complex subject than might appear at first sight. This can be illustrated by a single example.

Consider a timber window set in a prepared opening in a brick external wall. Unless the wall is to be built up around the window frame, in which case the frame itself will serve as a template for the opening, the architect will be faced with making the brick opening larger all round than the overall dimensions of the frame which is to be fitted into it; for otherwise it will be impossible, in practical terms, to insert the one into the other. It would seem that the joiner will need to work to one dimension and the bricklayer to another if a satisfactory fit is to be achieved. How, simply, is each to be instructed?

To answer 'dimension the frame 15 mm all round smaller than the opening' is unduly simplistic. Apart from the daunting prospect of trying to represent a series of 15 mm differences on a location plan at a scale of 1:100, the problem is compounded by inaccuracies which are bound to occur in both the fabrication of the frame and the erection of the brickwork, to say nothing of the difficulty of inserting one centrally into the other.

The co-ordinating dimension
The solution lies in the concept of the co-ordinating dimension, which may be defined as the distance between two hypothetical planes of reference—known as co-ordinating planes—representing the theoretical boundary between adjoining building elements. A diagrammatic indication of the window in the wall will clarify this definition (**3.9**).

The co-ordinating dimension is the one which will be shown on the location and assembly drawings, and is the nominal dimension to which both the bricklayer and joiner will work. If that dimension is 1500 mm, then we may speak quite properly of a '1500 opening' and of a '1500 window'. The nominal size of the frame will be reduced by the manufacturer to a size which is smaller all round by 10 mm, this being the dimension laid down by the British Woodworking Manufacturers' Association as an appropriate reduction for timber products in order to produce a final or 'work size'.

We now have a situation which may be shown diagrammatically, as in **3.10**.

It must be borne in mind, however, that neither the bricklayer nor the joiner is likely to achieve 100 per cent dimensional accuracy, and the best that can be done is to specify the degree of inaccuracy that will be regarded as acceptable.

In the present example two trades are involved and the degree of precision to be demanded must be realistically related to the nature of the materials in which they are working. It may be assumed that the bricklayer will set up a rough temporary timber framework as a simple template to which his brickwork may be built to form the opening. For the bricklayer, therefore, an opening which varies in size between x +15 mm and x −0 mm, with x being the co-ordinating dimension may be considered reasonable. In the timber component, however, it will be realistic to accept variation in size between y +5 mm and y −5 mm where y is the laid down work size of the component.

The final assembly of window and brickwork may therefore have two extreme dimensional situations, with a range of intermediate possibilities (**3.11**).

The selected method of sealing the gap between

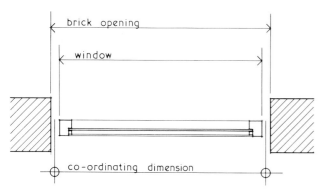

3.9 *The co-ordinating dimension*

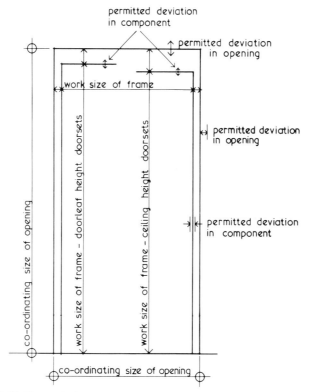

3.10 *The work size*

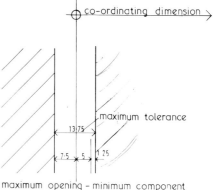
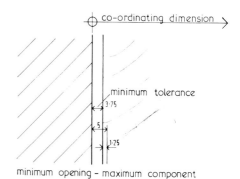

3.11 *Dimensional possibilities of window/wall assembly*

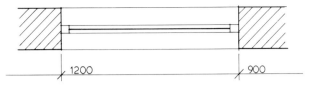

3.12 Opening on plan defined by its co-ordinating dimension

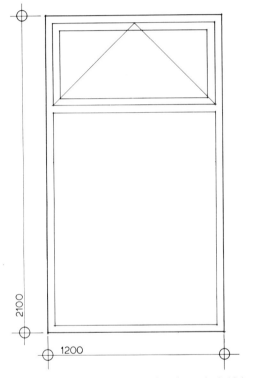

3.13 Component destined to fill the opening shown in 3.12 is also defined by its co-ordinating dimension.

component and opening must take account of these variables if it is to work in all situations. The sizing of components and the establishment of their work sizes and permitted deviations is a whole field for study in its own right. An obvious instance is that of pre-cast concrete cladding panels with a compressible extruded plastic section providing the weathertight seal between them where, unless great care is taken, the maximum permitted gap between panels may be too great to hold the plastic section in compression, while the minimum permitted gap is too small for it to be inserted. The UK Building Research Establishment's paper on 'Tolerance and Fit' is important reading in this connection.

The above discussion is intended as the most basic of introductions to a complex subject. But it may be seen how the whole of dimensioning practice becomes simplified by the concept of the co-ordinating dimension. The assembly of window and wall will be dimensioned on the location plan as in **3.12**, and if he is wise the architect will similarly designate the co-ordinating dimensions on his component drawing (**3.13**).

It will be prudent to note in the drawing set that this method has been adopted. A note on the component schedule or component drawings stating that 'Dimensions given for components are co-ordinating dimensions. The manufacturer is to make his own reductions to give the work size of the component.' should avoid the possibility of error.

Definitions
It may be helpful at this point to summarise some of the terms referred to into a list of definitions and to add to them others in common use:

Co-ordinating plane Line representing the hypothetical boundary between two adjoining building elements.

Co-ordinating dimension The distance between two co-ordinating planes.

Controlling dimension The key dimension—normally between co-ordinating planes—which is the crucial determining dimension in an assembly and which must remain sacrosanct while intermediate dimensions may be permitted some tolerance.

Work size The actual finished size of a component.

Permitted deviation (sometimes known as manufacturer's tolerance) The amount (plus or minus) by which the finished size of a component may vary from its stated work size and still be acceptable.

Dimension line The line drawn between two planes with a view to showing the dimension between them.

Extension line The line drawn from a plane which is to be dimensioned, and intersecting the dimension line.

Leader line The line joining a note with the object which is the subject of that note.

Dimensioning—some examples
Appendix 5, dealing with non-active lines, gives examples of the types of dimension line recommended for different purposes. The following comments may be helpful in establishing the correct approach to dimensioning such diverse drawings as the site plan, primary element location plans, location and assembly sections and component and sub-component details.

To set out a building it is necessary to establish a datum parallel to one of the building's axes. The criteria by which this datum is selected will vary. Where there is an improvement line required for the site, or an established building line, these will obviously be important starting points. If the site is relatively uncluttered then existing physical features—boundary fencing, adjoining buildings, etc—will be used. In certain specialised structures orientation may be the overriding factor.

The important thing is that the chosen starting points should be unambiguous and clearly recognisable on site.

It is better to establish the datum some distance from the perimeter of the new building so that it may be pegged in as a permanent record during construction. The building may then be set out from it by offsets. A datum which coincides with one of the new building's faces will be obliterated as soon as excavation starts.

Where the construction is load-bearing the setting out dimension from the datum should be given to the outside face of the wall. Where the structure is framed, this dimension should be to grid centre-line.

The dimensioning of the location plan shown in **3.14** is

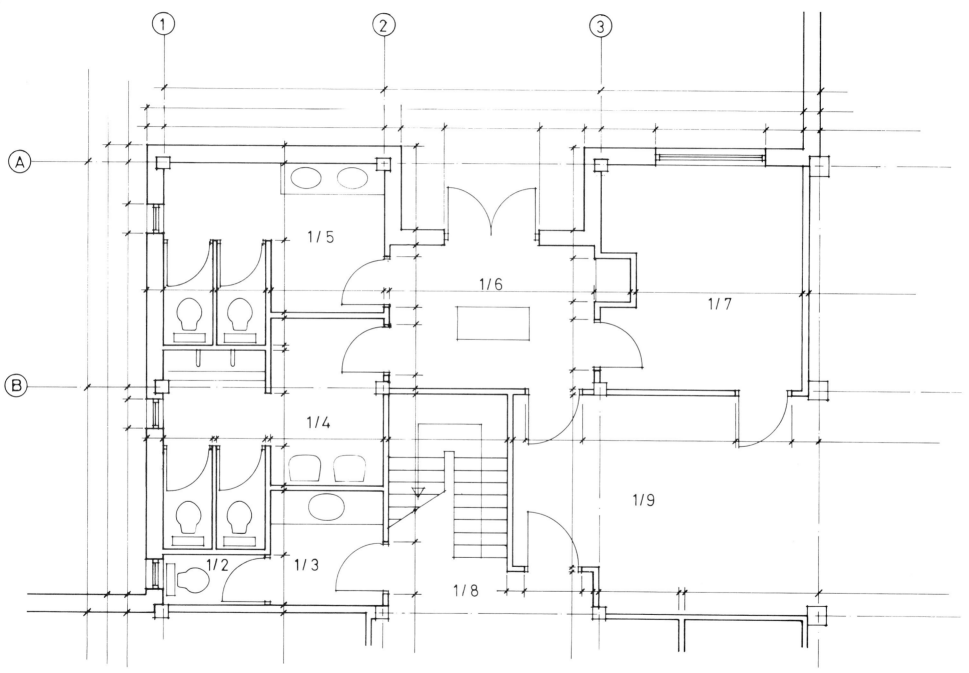

3.14 *Typical dimensioning of primary elements location plan. (The other location plans in the set will not need to record these dimensions)*

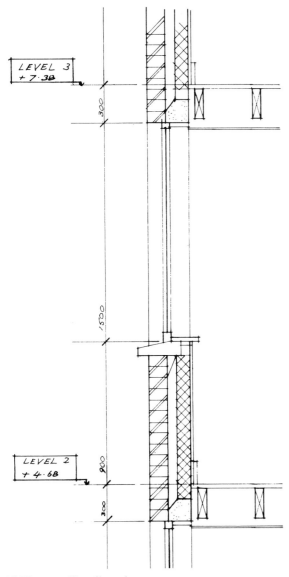

3.15 *The controlling dimension*

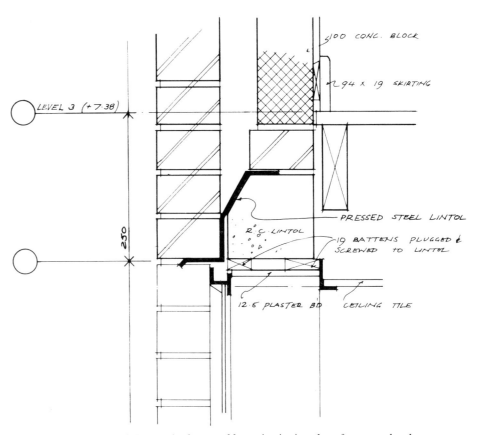

3.16 *Vertical location of elements in the assembly section is given by reference to the planes established in* **3.15**

largely self-explanatory. Note the three strips of dimensions along the external walls, the string picking up the grid being the outermost line of the three. Overall dimensions are included, partly as an arithmetical check for the dimensioner, partly to aid the estimator.

Generally speaking, internal setting out is effected by judiciously selected strings of dimensions. Where the positioning of a given element is critical, however, (where, for example, it must be a precise distance from a certain wall face) it has been dimensioned from that face alone, to ensure that the setter out works in a similar fashion. When it is critical that a feature be in the centre of a wall face an 'equal/equal' indication has been given from its centre line.

Figures **3.15** and **3.16** show the role of the controlling dimension in vertical setting out. The salient levels dimensioned from the relevant datum (in this case the finished floor level) in the location section appear again as reference planes in the larger scale detail. The only comment that needs to be made about components and sub-components is the general one that they should be dimensioned to their finished sizes. This is particularly relevant when the material involved is timber.

A note to the effect that the finished section is to be 'ex 150 × 50' is too imprecise for a constructional world of off-site fabrication. Economy requires that the finished section should realistically be obtainable from one of the standard sawn sections. To give a *finished* size of 150 × 50, for example, would result in the client paying for a large quantity of wood-shavings and sawdust.

Lettering

Hand lettering
The appearance of far too many carefully drawn sheets is marred by the quality of their lettering. This is a pity, because the cultivation of a rapid, legible and attractive lettering style is not difficult. All that it requires is a good model to serve as a guide and a great deal of practice.

Alternatives to hand lettering are available, but all are in their various ways time-consuming, inconvenient to add to or amend, and, when looked at in bulk, unattractive and lacking in character.

Five basic styles of hand lettering may be identified:
- upper case—upright
- upper case—sloping
- lower case—upright
- lower case—sloping
- cursive.

Examples of each are shown in **3.17**. They are not given as definitive statements of how to do it, for every draughtsman will impart his individual character to them, whether he intends to or not. Nevertheless, they may serve as good models of their respective kinds, and it will not be possible to move very far from them without irritating mannerisms and loss of legibility creeping in.

Which of the five styles to choose depends partly upon personal inclination, partly upon any policy of standardising format that an individual office may have. It should be noted, however, that on the whole upper case lettering tends to be more legible, and that most people find sloping lettering easier to execute than upright. Upright lettering looks very attractive when all of its vertical strokes are indeed upright, but it is easy for stray deviations from the vertical to creep in (nothing looks worse than letters which actually slope backwards). With forward sloping lettering marginal changes in angle are less noticeable.

Cursive lettering is probably the most rapid form of all, and provided that a good style is chosen and reasonable care taken to ensure that absolute legibility is always the main objective it serves well enough and lends character to a drawing.

It has its pitfalls, however. The normal handwriting of most people is not up to the job, and the deliberate acquisition of a new and more legible cursive style seems somewhat pointless. Bearing in mind the likelihood that further notes will need to be added to the drawing at a later date and by other hands which are unlikely to resemble the original very closely, it seems best to limit the use of cursive annotation to details likely to have a short life.

Figure **3.18** shows a recommended sequence of strokes in the formation of individual upper case letters. Increasing fluency and self-confidence (each generates the other) will enable the competent draughtsman to simplify this stroke-making procedure in due course into an acceptable and rapidly produced individual style.

Horizontal guidelines are essential unless the draughtsman is very experienced and skilful. They may be drawn lightly in pencil for subsequent erasure (when the lettering is in ink) or may take the form of a closely gridded sheet laid underneath the tracing paper.

Lettering for the purpose of general annotation should be a minimum of 2 mm in height for upper case letters and 1.5 mm in height for lower case, and with the latter, of course, the stems and tails of certain letters

3.17 *Examples of different types of hand lettering*

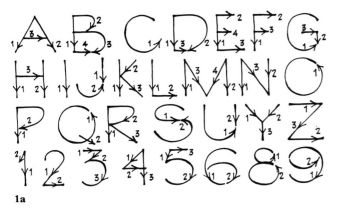

3.18 *Formation of the upper case alphabet*

will extend beyond this dimension. There is no theoretical maximum size, but certainly on most location and assembly drawings the amount of annotation likely to be required will scarcely fit on the sheet if sizes much in excess of the minimum are used.

The spacing between lines of upper case lettering should not be less than the size of the letters themselves. A 1:1 ratio is helpful when gridded underlays are being used.

With lower case lettering the spacing should be somewhat greater than the lettering size to avoid upstanding stems from one line coming into conflict with the tails of letters from the line above.

The thickness of line used for general annotation should be either 0.3 mm or 0.25 mm, depending upon which range of pen sizes is being adopted, and when pencil is being used the line should similarly approximate to these thicknesses. Lettering for titling and for coded references (room names and numbers, section references to other drawings, etc) should be slightly larger for added emphasis. 2.5:2 is a suitable ratio, and in the case of titles at least a heavier weight of line may be used. Be careful not to overwhelm the drawing however. The art of calligraphy is a subtle one.

Most lettering will normally run from left to right of the sheet and will be parallel to the bottom edge. When it becomes necessary for lettering to run vertically, it should always run from the bottom upwards. (This applies also to strings of dimensions.)

Notes should be placed reasonably close to the area to which they refer, but at all times make sure there is sufficient space for the note to be expanded subsequently if necessary. Notes of a general nature are better collected together in a convenient corner of the sheet.

Figure **3.19** is an example of well spaced out lettering on a quite complex detail. Note how a little forethought at all stages in the production of this plan has helped to ensure that notes, dimensions and coded references do not clash with each other or with the building.

Alternative lettering methods
Stencils: These are available in a wide range of sizes and styles, and include upper and lower case in both upright and sloping forms. If for any reason hand lettering is not used then stencils provide the most practical alternative, being relatively rapid to use. Their most sensible application is probably for those lettering aspects mentioned previously as benefiting from some slight emphasis.

Dry transfer letters are not recommended for working drawings for the same reason as dry transfer symbols. They are liable to come off with use, and in any case are relatively expensive and slow to apply.

Wide carriage typewriters: Wide carriage typewriters are a possibility, but since the drawing has to be taken from the drawing board for the lettering to be applied the sensible approach is for all the lettering to be added at the same time. Unless the draughtsman is also a competent typist, it is implicit that he must have prepared the notes in draft on a print of the drawing in order that a typist might add them to the negative in the correct positions. Since presumably the draft notes had to be prepared in a form legible enough for them to be read, it is difficult to understand why the draughtsman did not just put them on the negative in the first place.

Lettering machines: These are more flexible, in that they may be used at the drawing board, and indeed will fit onto a drafting machine or a parallel motion unit. Figure **3.20** shows one such device on the market.

Transparent film: A transparent film is marketed on which notes may be typed, and which is then cut up and stuck onto the negative. It may have uses in particular situations, but it suffers from the same disadvantage as the other non-manual methods of lettering—it is not related to the day-to-day exigencies of rapid working drawing production.

Title panels
The title panel should be at the bottom right-hand corner of the sheet, so that when the drawing is folded properly, the title and number are always clearly visible. Figure **3.21** shows the recommended method of folding various 'A'-sized sheets.

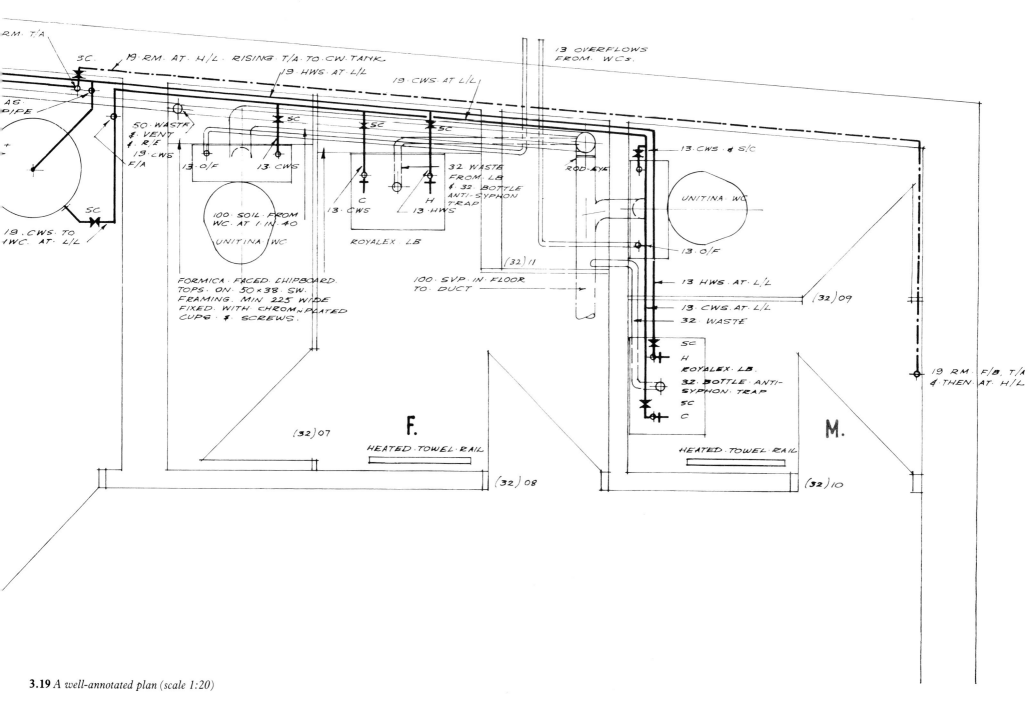

3.19 *A well-annotated plan (scale 1:20)*

The format of the panel will vary, but it must make provision for the following (minimum) information to be displayed:
- name, address and telephone number of the issuing office
- name of the client
- name and address of the project
- title of the drawing
- scale of the drawing
- date of first issue
- reference, description and dates of subsequent revisions.

Optionally, the panel may carry further information, such as the name of the project architect, the names of the persons preparing and checking the drawing, office job reference, etc.

Figure 3.22 shows a suitable format, but many are available.

Title panels may either be pre-printed on to standard drawing sheets or supplied in the form of adhesive and transparent printed panels for sticking to the back of the completed negative.

Trimming lines and margins are unnecessary when standard 'A'-size sheets are used, since copy paper for dyeline printing almost invariably comes pre-cut to size. It is useful, however, if the line marking the left-hand edge of the title panel continues up for the full extent of the sheet, since this reserves a strip along the side of the sheet for the addition of notes, revisions, etc.

When completing the title panel it is most important that the drawing title be stated simply and consistently, giving the casual searcher a brief but accurate and informative statement about the drawing's content. The following is a typical title which follows a logical pattern:

Location plan—level one primary elements.

3.20 *Commercially available lettering machine*

3.21 *Recommended method of folding 'A' size sheets always keeps the title panel visible*

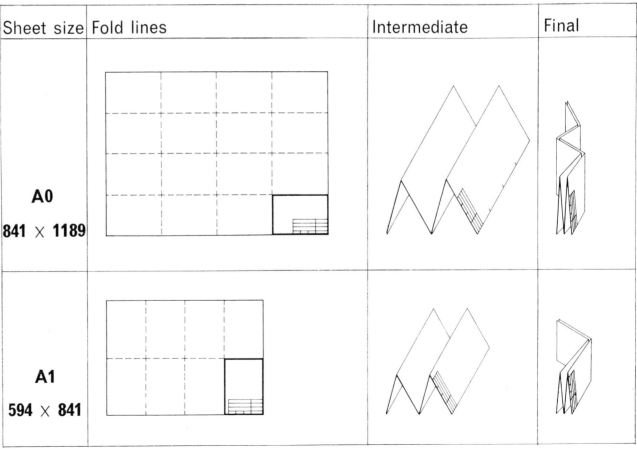

3.22 (Left) Example of drawing title panel

We are told, in sequence, that the drawing is in the location category; that it is a plan; the level at which the plan is taken; and, because this is an elementalised set of drawings, we are told finally the element which the drawing shows.

The identical title will appear in the drawing register.

Table IV The RIBA outline plan of work

Stage	Purpose of work and Decisions to be reached	Tasks to be done	People directly involved	Usual Terminology
A. Inception	To prepare general outline of requirements and plan future action.	Set up client organisation for briefing. Consider requirements, appoint architect.	All client interests, architect.	Briefing
B. Feasibility	To provide the client with an appraisal and recommendation in order that he may determine the form in which the project is to proceed, ensuring that it is feasible, functionally, technically and financially.	Carry out studies of user requirements, site conditions, planning, design, and cost etc., as necessary to reach decisions.	Clients' representatives, architects, engineers and QS according to nature of project.	
C. Outline Proposals	To determine general approach to layout, design and construction in order to obtain authoritative approval of the client on the outline proposals and accompanying report.	Develop the brief further. Carry out studies on user requirements, technical problems, planning, design and costs, as necessary to reach decisions.	All client interest, architects, engineers, QS and specialists as required.	Sketch Plans
D. Scheme Design	To complete the brief and decide on particular proposals, including planning arrangement appearance, constructional method, outline specification, and cost, and to obtain all approvals.	Final development of the brief, full design of the project by architect, preliminary design by engineers, preparation of cost plan and full explanatory report. Submission of proposals for all approvals.	All client interests, architects, engineers, QS and specialists and all statutory and other approving authorities.	

Brief should not be modified after this point

E. Detail Design	To obtain final decision on every matter related to design, specification, construction and cost.	Full design of every part and component of the building by collaboration of all concerned. Complete cost checking of designs.	Architects, QS, engineers and specialists, contractor (if appointed).	Working Drawings

Any further change in location, size, shape, or cost after this time will result in abortive work

F. Production Information	To prepare production information and make final detailed decisions to carry out work.	Preparation of final production information i.e. drawings, schedules and specifications.	Architects, engineers and specialists, contractor (if appointed).	
G. Bills of Quantities	To prepare and complete all information and arrangements for obtaining tender.	Preparation of Bills of Quantities and tender documents.	Architects, QS, contractor (if appointed).	
H. Tender Action	Action as recommended in paras. 7–14 inclusive of 'Selective Tendering'*	Action as recommended in paras. 7–14 inclusive of 'Selective Tendering'*	Architects, QS, engineers, contractor, client.	
J. Project Planning	Action in accordance with paras. 5–10 inclusive of 'Project Management'*	Action in accordance with paras. 5–10 inclusive of 'Project Management'*	Contractor, sub-contractors.	Site Operations
K. Operations on site	Action in accordance with paras. 11–14 inclusive of 'Project Management'*	Action in accordance with paras. 11–14 inclusive of 'Project Management'*	Architects, engineers, contractors, sub-contractors, QS, client.	
L. Completion	Action in accordance with paras. 15–18 inclusive of 'Project Management'*	Action in accordance with paras. 15–18 inclusive of 'Project Management'*	Architects, engineers, contractor, QS, client.	
M. Feed-Back	To analyse the management, construction and performance of the project.	Analysis of job records. Inspections of completed building. Studies of building in use.	Architects, engineers, QS, contractor, client.	

* Publication of National Joint Consultative Council of Architects, Quantity Surveyors and Builders.

4 Working drawing management

The objective

Prior to this chapter production information has been the primary concern. It is this information—both drawings and specification—which represents the final commitment to paper of planning and constructional decisions arrived at during the earlier stages of the project. This final documentation is inevitably a time-consuming process, and if it is to be carried through smoothly and economically it is important that all the necessary decisions should have been taken before its commencement.

It is also true to say that of all the aspects of an architect's work it is this final documentation that lends itself best to the deployment of a team. On very few projects will there be the time available to allow the working drawings to be prepared by a single individual, and in practice even quite small buildings will involve more than one person at this stage.

The objective, therefore, is the achievement of a rapid, well-programmed draw-up, in which the information to be documented by each member of the team is allocated in advance with due reference to his experience and ability, and during which only the most routine and undemanding of technical problems should remain for resolution. In order to achieve this it is important that a more or less rigid adherence to the plan of work is maintained.

The plan of work

The RIBA Plan of Work was illustrated at the beginning of this book as constituting the basic discipline within which the manifold activities of the architect are contained. It is shown on p. 83 as Table IV, and against each stage have been noted the major aspects of the work dealt with at that stage which will have a bearing on the working drawing process, or which will be influenced by it.

The plan of work is sometimes criticised as being doctrinaire and unrelated to the harsh facts of professional life. Certainly in practice there are constant pressures to do things out of sequence because there is a short-term benefit to be gained by doing so. It is very tempting when struggling with knotty problems of detailing, or seemingly lethargic fellow consultants, to take the view that a premature start on the final drawings will in some way have a cathartic effect on the enterprise.

But 'time spent on reconnaissance is seldom wasted' is a military adage that is valid in other fields; a proper laying of the groundwork will help to avoid those drawing office crises, destructive alike of morale and financial budgeting, when a team of several people is brought to a standstill by the sudden realisation of some unresolved problem.

From the standpoint of stage F then let us first look back to the preceding stages, where a little forethought will make life in the subsequent stages a great deal easier.

Pre-requisites for stage F

There is a basic minimum of information which needs to be available before embarking on stage F, and this should certainly include the following:
- final design set of drawings (stage D)
- record of statutory approvals (stages D and E)
- key detailing in draft (stage E)
- room data sheets (stages C to E)
- outline specification
- applicable trade literature
- library of standard details
- drawing register
- design team network
- drawing office programme.

These items are dealt with in detail below.

Final design set (stage D)

It will always be necessary to produce a properly drawn set of drawings showing the final design, and if subsequent changes are called for, no matter how minor, it is sensible to record these on the negatives themselves rather than in any other form, so that at any one time there exists an up-to-date record, and confirmation, of what has been agreed with the client. Obviously these will be presentation drawings, prepared in the manner best calculated to obtain the client's approval. Nevertheless before the trees and the shadows are added, it is prudent to take a set of copy negatives from the unadorned masters, for then definitive plans and elevations will be available which may be issued immediately to other consultants on commencement of stage E, and the rather fruitless business often encountered of re-drawing the whole scheme as 'draft working drawings' once design approval has been obtained may be eliminated, with benefit to both office economics and programme.

This implies, of course, that the scales and draughting techniques adopted should be compatible with use for both purposes, but this is quite feasible if the subsequent use is borne in mind from the outset (**4.1** and **4.2**).

Statutory approvals
A chicken and egg situation, this one—you can't get approval until you've submitted the drawing: you can't prepare the drawing until you've got approval. But visits to the fire officer and the building inspector in the early stages of the scheme will not only set up lines of communication which will be invaluable for the future, but will establish principles for incorporation in subsequent detailing. It is a firming-up process. It is essential to know at the start of stage C the spacing of escape stairs the fire officer will demand, and by the end of it their widths. It is essential to know before the end of stage E the required fire rating of all doors. Nobody should need to raise such questions in the middle of stage F.

The decision and agreements must be recorded, of course, and it is obviously more helpful to give someone a marked up drawing to work from than a bulky file to read. The final design drawings referred to above as being issued to consultants form an obvious basis for the recording of this sort of information (**4.3**).

Key detailing in draft (stage E)
At the completion of stage E there should be a carefully thought out solution available for every construction problem that can be envisaged, and this will involve the production of a sheaf of draft details in which the principles of these solutions are established.

The drafts will not be elaborated into final drawings. They will remain as source documents, and the decisions they embody will be fed out into various stage F drawings—location sections, assemblies and component details—and the specification.

It should be noted in particular how the one draft assembly section generates a whole series of detailed statements about various aspects of the building. In an earlier day it might have been thought adequate to issue the section as a final drawing, a 'typical detail' from which the operative might be expected to infer detailed variations to suit differing but basically similar situations throughout the building. In today's very different conditions this is just not adequate.

It is, however, reasonable to expect a drawing office assistant to apply the principles involved to other aspects of the building, which he will either identify or which will be identified for him by others with greater experience or knowledge of the particular building.

This approach to detailing, whereby the basic principles of construction are established by the principal or the project architect but are translated into detailed practice by an assistant, lends itself to considerable drawing office economies. By defining the necessary drawing office tasks at the outset of the programme (a subject which will be dealt with in detail later) the appropriate level of responsibility may be set for all members of the team.

Room data sheets
The advantages of room by room scheduling as a medium for conveying information about internal finishes and fittings have been noted earlier. The gradual collection during stage E of such information into a source document of comparable format will clearly assist in the preparation of such schedules at stage F. Whether this is done on a print of the floor plan, or on a series of individual sheets representing each room or room type is a decision which will be made in the light of the size and complexity of the individual project. At the end of the day there will exist, hopefully, a complete record of each room's requirements, with indications where applicable as to the authority for those requirements, serving alike as a detailed record of client instructions and a briefing manual and check list when the final documentation is being prepared.

Outline specification
The case is argued elsewhere in this handbook for a specification which is an integral part of the production documentation rather than the afterthought which puzzled foremen often assume it to have been. If drawings are to be freed of the detailed written descriptions they are frequently made to carry, it is implicit that this information must be conveyed to the contractor by other means. Indeed, the philosophy of the National Building Specification is reliant upon the geometry of the building and of its component parts being covered by the drawings, with selection from alternative materials and definition of quality standards being covered by the specification.

It is desirable therefore that both drawings and specification should draw their information from a common source document, and that this document should be produced before the stage F programme gets under way.

The outline specification is a useful format for this document, partly because something approaching it will have been needed by the quantity surveyor for his final design stage cost check to have any validity. It consists basically of a check list (CI/SfB elemental order is a convenient framework) upon which decisions on construction and materials may be noted as they are made.

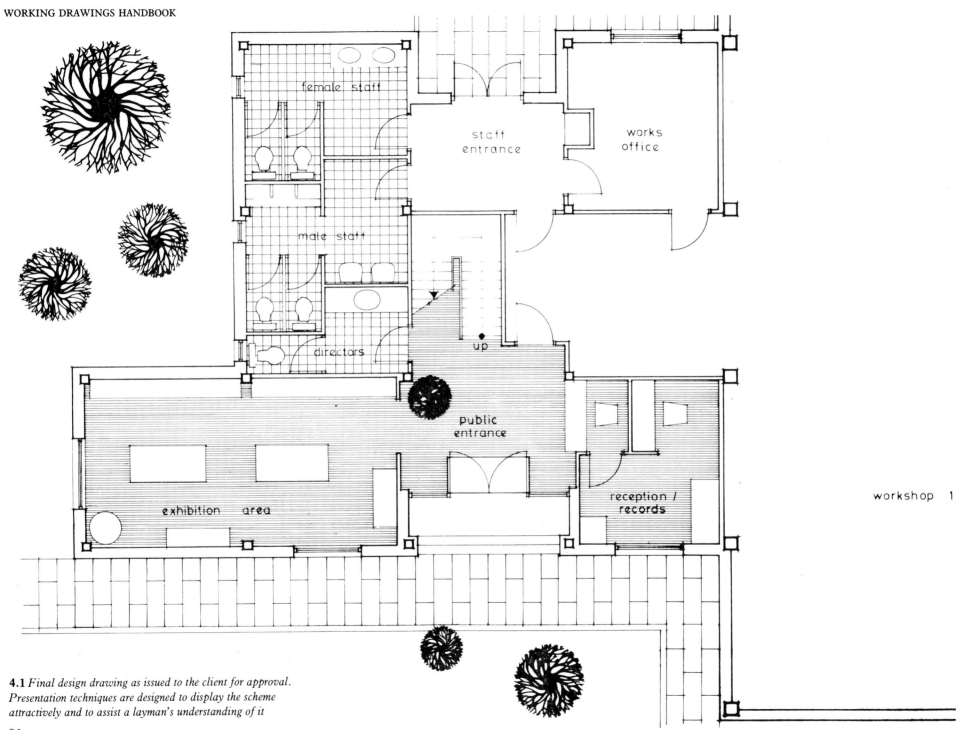

4.1 *Final design drawing as issued to the client for approval. Presentation techniques are designed to display the scheme attractively and to assist a layman's understanding of it*

WORKING DRAWING MANAGEMENT

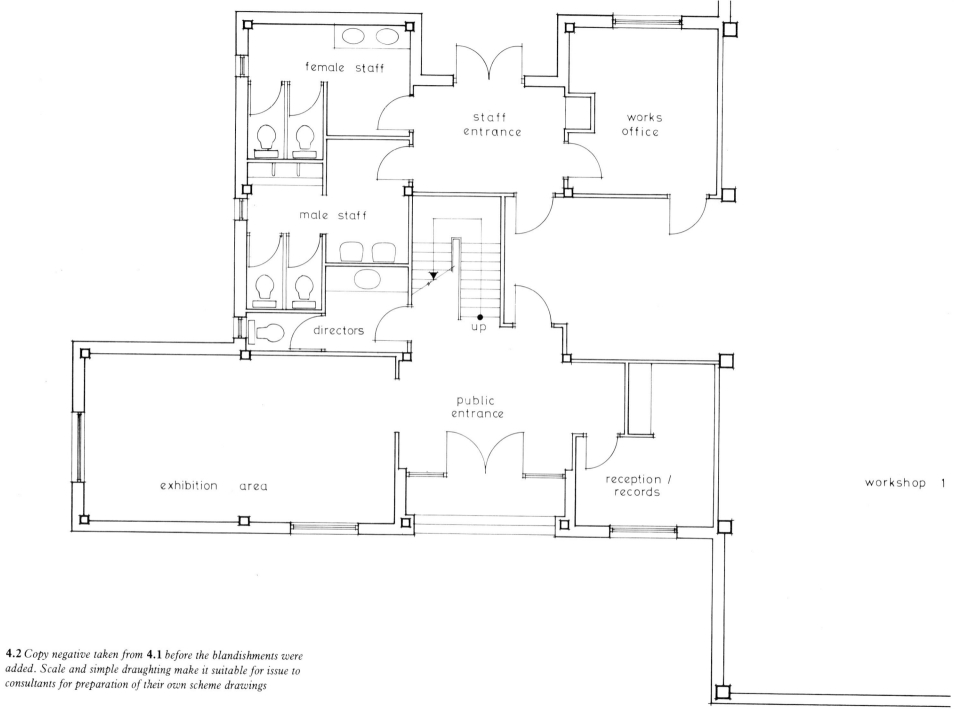

4.2 *Copy negative taken from* **4.1** *before the blandishments were added. Scale and simple draughting make it suitable for issue to consultants for preparation of their own scheme drawings*

WORKING DRAWINGS HANDBOOK

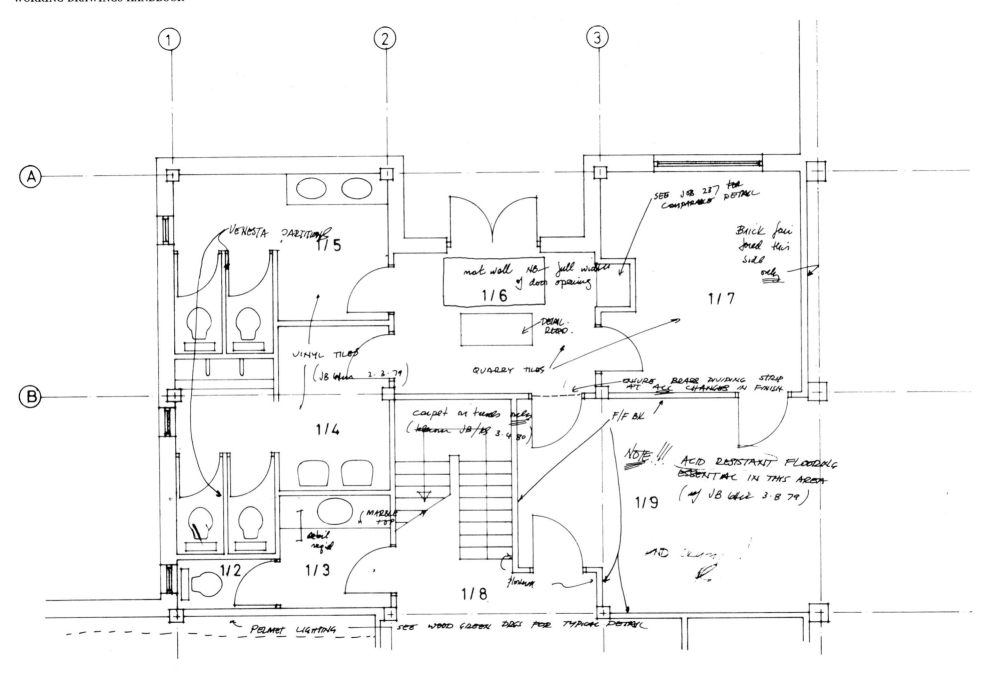

4.3 *Print taken from* **4.2** *and marked up as a briefing guide to the drawing office at Stage E*

WORKING DRAWING MANAGEMENT

Formalising these decisions into such a document at an early stage ensures that they are made at the proper level of experience. Readers of *The Honeywood File* will recall Ridoppo, the wonder paint that crept off the walls and out of the house. We have all had our Ridoppos, but at least it ought to be possible to ensure that they are not selected by the drawing office junior at the last minute because time was short and nobody had told him any better.

Trade literature

The rationalised drawing structure provides a convenient framework on which to hang manufacturers' literature. There is no virtue in redrawing the builders' work details printed in Bloggs & Company's catalogue when a photocopy suitably overcoded with the job and drawing number will convey the information more cheaply and accurately. (Bloggs & Company are not likely to object to the resultant wider distribution of their literature.)

But in any case the literature which it is known will be required, if only as source documents for one's own drawings, should be assembled early in the day. It can be frustrating to have to interrupt work on a detail to telephone for urgently needed trade literature and then wait two or three days for its arrival (**4.4**).

Library of standard details

A lot of practices attempt at some point in their existence to crystallise the accumulated wisdom and experience of the practice into a set of standard details, only to find with increasing disillusionment as they proceed that not nearly so much is really standard as was at first supposed, and that the very existence of a standard drawing which is nearly (but not quite) applicable to the project in hand is a dangerous inducement to compromise.

On the other hand it is frustrating to realise that the detail being worked out laboriously in one room for project A is not going to end up significantly different

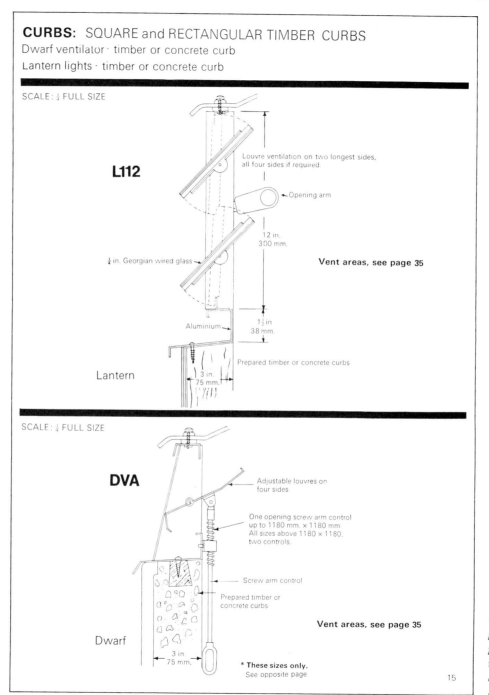

4.4 *Manufacturer's catalogue giving precise fixing details. It is pointless to re-draw this information when the catalogue can be issued to the contractor as an instruction*

1 Advise team of outcome of Stage D report
2 Maintain and co-ordinate progress.
3 Provide outstanding information, avoiding abortive work.
4 Complete outstanding user studies.
5 Up-date Stage D information for briefing meeting.
6 Up-date Stage D information for briefing meeting.
7 Up-date Stage D information for briefing meeting.
8 Up-date Stage D information for briefing meeting.
9 State policy requirements for construction and finishes.
10 Confirm tender and contract policies.
11 Convene briefing meeting.
12 Review Job Control Plan for this stage.
13 Prepare draft activity programme.
14 Hold briefing meeting and agree the following: roles and responsibilities; elements for detail design; project divisions; scales for location drawings.
15 Complete location drawings to agreed scale and distribute.
16 Decide all matters put up for decision at any time.
17 Prepare detailed work analysis.
18 Prepare detailed work analysis.
19 Prepare detailed work analysis.
20 Complete activity programme.
21 Hold programme meeting. Discuss work analysis, location drawings, agree element solutions and alternatives.
22 Explore solutions in collaboration with team.
23 Explore solutions in collaboration with team.
24 Explore solutions in collaboration with team.
25 Consult suppliers and manufacturers as necessary.
26 Cost check alternatives and compare with cost plan.
27 Consider alternatives and report to meeting.
28 Hold meeting to agree solutions for development. Eliminate alternatives.
29 Obtain approval as necessary to selected solutions.
30 Hold further consultation with statutory authorities on principles of construction.
31 Provide team with preliminary information on adopted solution.
32 Provide team with preliminary information on adopted solution.
33 Provide team with preliminary information on adopted solution.
34 Develop solutions with typical details in collaboration with team.
35 Develop solutions with typical details in collaboration with team.
36 Develop solutions with typical details in collaboration with team.
37 Obtain preliminary estimates as necessary.
38 Co-ordinate information and add to location drawings.
39 Cost check developed solutions (main cost check).
40 Discuss and agree developed solutions and cost.
41 Receive details of final cost check if necessary.
42 Prepare outstanding specification clauses.
43 Adjust if necessary and finalise all details including layout drawings.
44 Adjust if necessary and finalise all details including layout drawings.
45 Adjust if necessary and finalise all details including layout drawings.
46 Co-ordinate information and add to location drawings.
47 Adjust costs as necessary.
48 Review final drawings and cost.
49 Collect and check all final drawings.
50 Apply for Building Regulations approval.
51 Review planning consent and re-apply if necessary.
52 Agree or confirm: contract conditions procedure of information to tender, list of contractors and nominated sub-contractors, advance ordering e.g. demolition, piling, steelwork, etc.
53 Prepare proposals for sequence of information required for B of Qs.
54 Hold briefing meeting and agree: rules and responsibilities, drawing format, scale, practical divisions, use of copy negatives; general requirements for cost flow; review of outstanding Approvals and Consents; review of Job Control Plan.
55 Prepare and distribute draft activity programme for Stage F.
56 Study draft Stage F programme and prepare comments.
57 Hold briefing meeting. Consider and agree or amend draft activity programme.
58 Finalise activity programme and distribute.

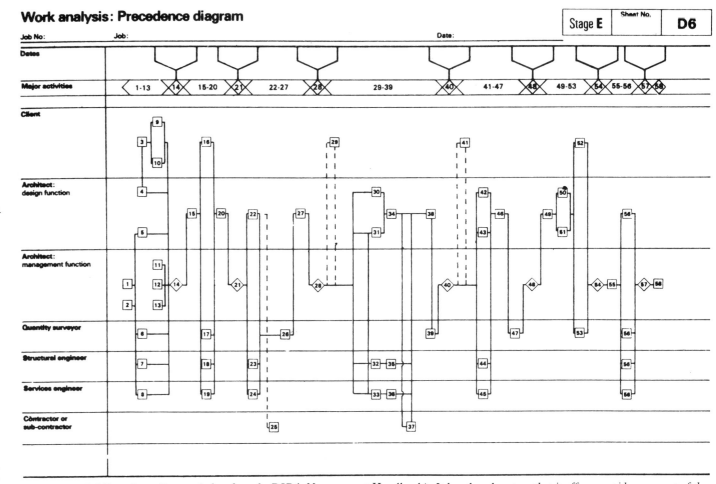

4.5 *Precedence diagram (taken from the RIBA Management Handbook). It has the advantage that it offers a rapid assessment of the consequences of any programme change, by its compatibility with computer analysis*

from the detail simultaneously being worked up across the corridor for project B. There should be room somewhere for a common-sense approach which does not attempt too much.

In practice few assembly details can be drawn so 'neutrally' as to render them directly re-usable on more than one project. The best that can be achieved in this field is to collect together drawings for various projects which embody solutions to recurring problems of principle, making them available for reference rather than direct re-use.

Component drawings are another matter, however, and provided that the office is using a structured drawing method it should be possible for each project to contribute its quota of contractor-made components (there is no point in re-drawing proprietary items) to a

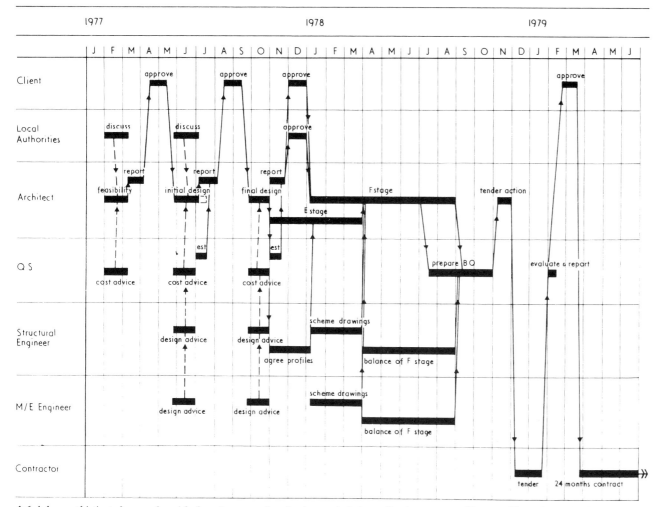

4.6 *A less sophisticated network, with the advantage that the time scale is immediately apparent. More readily understandable by the average client (and architect?) than a computer print-out*

central library. Such components as door-sets, shelving, cupboard fitments and external works items—bollards, fencing, etc—are suitable subjects for treatment.

The details, once selected for a standard library, should sensibly be re-numbered to ensure that when re-used on new projects they do not conflict with the numbering sequence for that project. C(32)501 for example might well be the first drawing in a library of internal joinery components, and would not conflict with component details specific to the project and numbered C(32)001, etc.

Design team programme
It is essential for the work of the entire design team to be integrated into a comprehensive programme, and unless a specialist programmer forms part of the team (and this is almost a *sine qua non* for any very large or complex projects) then the management role of team co-ordinator falls to the architect. Of all the consultant team he is probably best fitted by virtue of his training and his other duties to exercise the skills required, and should take advantage of his position as team leader to establish the appropriate procedures at the outset (see the section 'Design team meeting' on p 103).

In setting down the programme on paper, it will be found that a simple network is the best format, where the dependencies of the various team members upon each other may need to be shown. The format suggested in the RIBA Management Handbook *Guide on Resource Control* is one way to do it (**4.5**).

Its complexity may be unnecessarily daunting for the small to medium size project, however, particularly when a non-technical client is involved (the method is best suited to computer analysis and critical path method which may not be available). A simplified version on which a visual time scale has been superimposed will serve the same purpose in most cases (**4.6**).

The point to be reiterated is that every job, no matter how small, benefits from thoughtful programming, and the things to watch which are common to any method you use are:
• Restrict the network to as few activities as you reasonably can, paying particular attention to those activities whose completion is a pre-requisite for subsequent action by others. The purpose of the network is to provide each member of the team with basic management information. (He may well wish to develop for his own purposes a more detailed network of his own activities within the team management's framework.)
• Draw it simply. Its value as a document is that it can respond rapidly to a changed situation, and it must always be a realistic statement of the current position if it is to retain its credibility. It is no use having a programme drawn so beautifully that no one has the heart to re-draw it when it becomes out of date.

- Involve the client. Many of his activities are critical ones, particularly his formal approvals at various stages in the design, and he must be made aware of his responsibilities at the outset, along with the other members of the design team.

Planning the set
The structure of the final production set of drawings is central to both the smooth running of the project on site and the economics of the office producing it. It must therefore be considered in some detail.

Location drawings
Location plans: Given that the set is to be structured in the manner recommended in the earlier chapters the first decision to be made (and as noted earlier it will have been sensible to make it before preparation of the final design drawings) relates to sheet size and scale of the location plans. Basically the choice lies between a scale of 1:50, permitting a relatively large amount of information to be conveyed on a single sheet, or 1:100 where a greater degree of elementalisation will be required if the sheet is to remain uncluttered and legible, and where its main purpose is to provide a ready indication of where other and more detailed information is to be found.

A number of considerations will determine this decision, but they will centre around the size and complexity of the project. Housing and conversions are normally best carried out at the larger scale. Larger projects are often better suited to an elementalised set of 1:100 plans. This is partly because it allows reference back to detailed information which in many cases will be repetitive and which it would be uneconomical to redraw several times, and partly because it makes it easier to deploy a drawing team.

So most projects on which more than one draughtsman is likely to be engaged will benefit from the latter approach.

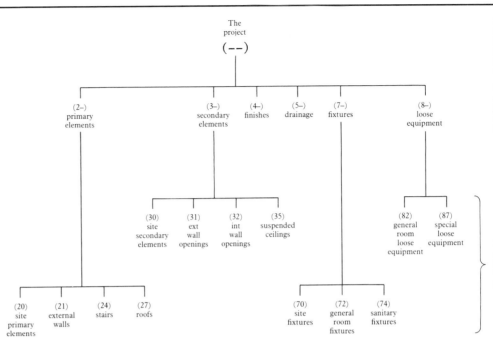

Table V A typical range of CI/SfB codes used on a large project

This band will normally be used for location drawings and a large number of the assembly drawings on small projects; for basic location plans (ie before process negatives are taken) on large projects

This band will normally cover the elementalised location plans on most projects. It will also be used for assembly and component coding on small projects

This band will normally cover assembly and component details and schedules on most projects, but may well be found unnecessarily detailed for small projects

In the discussion that follows it will be assumed that a single multi-storied building of some £500,000 contract value is being dealt with, that a drawing team of three/four people will be involved, and that the decision has been made to produce 1:100 location plans, elementalised for clarity.

The first allocation of sheets therefore will be to location plans, one sheet for each plan level. They will be coded L(– –) ie 'The project in general', because they are the basic drawings from which will be taken the copy negatives which will form the basis for subsequent elemental development. (As has been noted in chapter 2, numbering of those plans by floor levels is a refinement which, apart from possessing a certain elegance for the system-minded, offers eventual benefits to the site staff.)

The basic plans having been established it is necessary to consider what elemental plans should spring from them. The CI/SfB project manual offers a sensible method for identifying these. The complete range of elements in CI/SfB table 1 is available, and offers a useful check list (see table II on p 20).

Generally speaking, however, few projects—and then only those containing problems of a specialised nature—will need to go beyond the much more limited range shown in table V.

Other location drawings: Site plan, elevations and basic sections complete the set of location drawings. The complexity of the external works will influence the decision on whether or not to put all location information on a single drawing, but this is an area where co-ordination of information is of paramount importance and this may outweigh the other advantages inherent in the elemental approach.

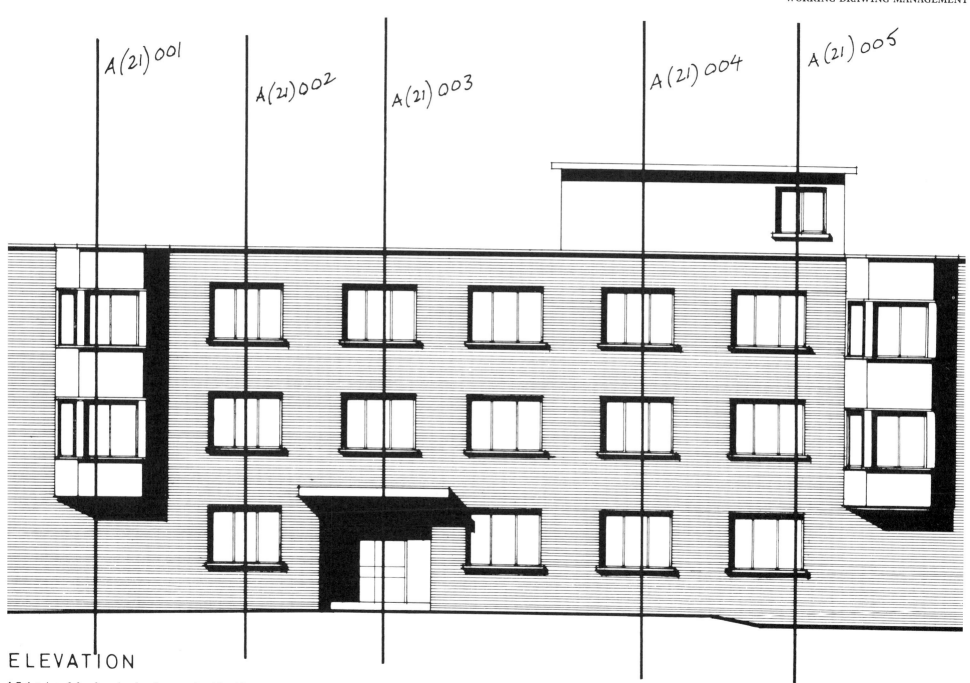

4.7 *A print of the elevation has been used to identify every section through the external walls where the construction changes (see p. 95)*

Peter Leach Associates — REGISTER OF **PRODUCTION** DRAWINGS

DRAWING CATEGORY

SHEET No.

TOTAL OF SHEETS IN CATEGORY

PROJECT No.

TITLE

Size	C1/Sfb	Number	Rev.	Description	Status	Remarks

CONTINUED ON SHEET No.

Columns Revision and Status are to be completed in pencil for up-dating.
The following codes are used:

1. **Drawing Category**

   L = Location Drawing
   A = Assembly Drawing
   C = Component Drawing
   S = Sub-Component Drawing
   IN = Information Drawing

2. **Drawing Status**

   E = Detail Design Drawing
   F = Final Production Drawing
   G = Drawing Reconciled with B.Q.
   K = Construction Drawing
   M = As Constructed Drawing

WORKING DRAWING MANAGEMENT

Location sections: These are best identified from the final design drawings. The external envelope of the building will generate the majority and the most important of these so the approach illustrated in **4.7** is useful. Bearing in mind that the approach initially is in terms of strictly limited strip sections rather than the traditional '½in section through the building', work systematically round the elevations, marking on a print the necessity for a fresh section every time the condition changes. You will finish with a series of L(21) details—desirably at a scale of 1:50—whose function will be to establish all important vertical dimensions and to provide references to larger scale (and largely repetitive) assembly details of head, cill and eaves, etc.

The location drawings have now been covered, and table VI lists them as they would appear in the drawing register.

Assemblies, components and schedules
The assembly drawings, component drawings and schedules appropriate to a project of this nature are listed in table VII.

The drawing register
The drawing register is a key document in the proper organisation of a working drawing project and as such needs to be something rather more than the loose sheet of paper with a scribbled list of drawing numbers and titles which sometimes suffices. After all, it serves a multitude of purposes, being at various times a declaration of intent, a record of performance, and, in the event of dispute on abandonment of the project after commencement of the working drawings, possibly a legal document.

In any case, it will have a relatively long and hard life, so it should be housed in a hardback folder or file, preferably of a colour striking enough to make it easily identifiable in the drawing office (it is essential that it be to hand immediately whenever a drawing is completed) and in a loose leaf format so that sheets may be removed and inserted easily. A4 is the obvious size, and **4.8** illustrates a useful format.

4.8 *A useful format for the drawing register. The explanatory notes help site staff as well as the drawing office*

It is strongly recommended that the register be prepared at the beginning of the working drawing programme, immediately the approximate list of required drawings has been identified. Its sequence of entries, therefore, will be similar to that of the hypothetical list of drawings and schedules given in Tables VI and VII; that is to say, it will be divided into location, assembly, component and schedule categories, and a separate sheet will be given to each CI/SfB element used. In consequence, there will be a relatively large number of sheets in the register, but the advantage will be that the bones of the drawing structure are laid out for all to see, in strict numerical sequence, and that if subsequently the need for a fresh drawing is identified (and the initial identification is unlikely to be accurate to within 5 per cent) then it may be entered without disruption either of the drawing numbering sequence, or of the register's own page order.

Within this framework the make-up of the individual register sheet may vary, but the information it should provide will consist of, at the minimum:
1. Drawing category—ie location, assembly, component or schedule.
2. Drawing element—its CI/SfB number, or other coded reference.
3. Drawing number—its unique identification within the category and element.
4. Revision suffix—sensibly added in pencil to facilitate revision.
5. Scale—not essential to the record, but can be helpful.
6. Size of sheet—because A4 and A1 drawings are unlikely to be stored in the same container, and the searcher must be told where to look. One test of the effectiveness of a drawing retrieval system is that it should always be quicker to locate the given drawing in the register and then go to it straight away than to leaf hopefully through the vertifile.

The date of completion and the dates of any revisions are not included, for they will be recorded on the drawing itself. Neither is it desirable to use the drawing register as a record of drawing issues. In the first place this practice imposes an administrative strain on the drawing office, which is likely to react unfavourably to seemingly bureaucratic procedures. In the second place, there is really very little to be gained from such a record. A check on drawing issues should be possible from other in-built procedures, such as standard drawing circulation lists, or drawing issue sheets.

Status coding
As has been noted earlier, many drawings perform different functions at different stages in their life, and some system of identifying their function at a given moment is a useful adjunct to a coding system.

One such method is to use the letter reference of the appropriate RIBA stage of work in conjunction with the drawing number, as a pencilled prefix:
E Detail design drawing. Any working drawing up until the time it is frozen for issue to the quantity surveyor when it becomes:
F Production drawing. Issued to the quantity surveyor who, during measurement, produces his own query list, picking up discrepancies, additional information required, etc. When these comments have been incorporated in the drawing, it becomes:
G Drawing reconciled with bill of quantities. That is the stage at which the drawing forms part of a tender set (**4.9**). It may not be released for construction, however, until it becomes:
K Construction drawing. Finally, and where the need for record drawings justifies it, the drawing becomes:
M As constructed.

> THIS DRAWING WAS USED IN THE PREPARATION OF THE BILLS OF QUANTITIES.
>
> ALL REVISIONS LISTED BELOW THIS LINE HAVE BEEN MADE SINCE THE BILLS OF QUANTITIES WERE PREPARED.

4.9 *Status coding of a drawing indicates only its status at the present time. This stamp freezes the drawing at the point when it relates to the other contract documents and is invaluable in controlling the contract*

Table VI Location drawings listed as they would appear in the drawing register

Drawing number	Scale	Title	Comments
L (——) 001 002 003 004 005	1 : 100	Plan at level 1—Basic 2— ,, 3— ,, 4— ,, 5— ,,	These are the basic floor plans from which copy negatives will be taken for development by the architect and other consultants into elemental location plans. Numbering of plans by levels aids retrieval of elementalised location information and offers a useful framework for identifying scheduled components, eg (31) 2/11, identifies external (window) opening no 11 on level 2. Location plans in their basic form will not be issued for construction purposes.
L(——) 006–009 010–013	1 : 100 1 : 100	Elevations 6, 7, 8, 9—Basic Sections 10, 11, 12, 13—Basic	Similar basic drawings of elevations and sections. Composite drawing numbering, eg 006–009, enables unique identification of each of several drawings on the same sheet. Eg the second elevation may be referred to simply as L (——) 007, rather than 'detail no 2 on drawing L (——) 006'. Sections are skeletal only and confined to giving a datum for each of the plan levels and giving a general picture only to the contractor.
L (——) 014	1 : 200	Site plan	The site plan is the only L (——) drawing to contain elemental information and to be issued for construction purposes, although the L (——) elevation and sections will be issued for the contractor's background information.
L (2–) 001 002 003 004 005	1 : 100	Plan at level 1—Primary elements 2— ,, 3— ,, 4— ,, 5— ,,	The key set of location plans giving dimensioned setting out information about the building. Note that while it would have been quite possible and perfectly in accordance with CI/SfB logic to split the information carried on these (2–) plans into (21) external walls, (22)—internal walls, (23)—floors, (24—stairs, (27)—roof and (28)—frame, common sense and the straightforward nature of the project suggested that a single (2–) grouping of these elements would suffice.
L (2–) 015–020	1 : 50	Location sections—External walls	The key location sections described earlier. They could equally well be coded (21) since they deal specifically with the external walls, but in either case their numbering commences at 15 to preserve the integrity of the numbering system. Again, 'Drawing L (2–) 015–020' provides a unique identification for each section.
L (3–) 001 002 003 004 005	1 : 100	Plan at level 1—Secondary elements 2— ,, 3— ,, 4— ,, 5— ,,	This series is used in this particular set as a means of locating, and uniquely identifying for scheduling purposes, internal doors, rooflights, gulleys and balustrades. While the plans group all this information under the (3–) code nevertheless the referencing of individual components will be more specific, eg plans L (3–), will locate and identify

Table VI (continued)

Drawing Number	Scale	Title	Comments
L (3–) 006–009	1 : 100	Elevations 6, 7, 8, 9—Secondary elements	both (32) 2/007 (internal opening, ie door number 7 on level 2) and (34) 003 (balustrade number 3). External openings, ie windows, external doors, ventilation grilles, etc, are located and numbered on these elevations. Note that while suspended ceiling (35) may also be included on the L (3–) series if required it may be less confusing to give them a separate (35) series of plans. Again common sense will dictate the approach.
L (4–) 001 002 003 004 005	1 : 100	Plan at level 1—Finishes	There are many ways of indicating the finishes you want. You may tabulate them into a purely descriptive schedule. You may code them into a form of shorthand (eg F3 = Floor finish type 3) and refer them back from the location plans to a vocabulary of finishes. (This is the method assumed in this set. It has the advantage that a drawn vehicle for the information already exists, ie the location plans, and the elemental method allows decisions on finishes to be deferred without detriment to other more urgent information being conveyed to the contractor at the right time.) Or you may use the room data sheets already referred to, with the advantage that this approach is more consistent with the room-by-room way in which finishing tradesmen actually work. The elevations are an obvious medium for conveying information about external finishes, and their representation may vary from Letratone to laboriously drawn brick coursing. NBS offers a more precise and less onerous alternative with its system of coded references tied back to comprehensive specification descriptions, F11/1 for example will be uniquely designated in the specification as 'the selected facing brick laid in 1:1:6 cement-lime-sand mortar in Flemish Bond and with flush pointing' and the coding F11/1 on the elevation will delineate the areas to which this description applies.
L (4–) 006–009	1 : 100	Elevations 6, 7, 8, 9—External finishes	
L (7–) 001 002 003 004 005	1 : 100	Plan at level 1—Fixtures 2— ,, 3— ,, 4— ,, 5— ,,	Self-explanatory, although it might be questioned what fixtures would appear on level 5 (roof). In this case, the (7–) coding was used to cover window cleaning track. And a flag pole.
L (8–) 001 002 003 004 005	1 : 100	Plan at level 1—Loose equipment 2— ,, 3— ,, 4— ,, 5— ,,	This coding seems to cover a multitude of omissions in practice. Mirrors, notice boards, fire exit signs, fire extinguishers—all tend to get added late in the life of a project. Rather than re-issuing cluttered-up and dog-eared amended copies of other plans, it is preferable to reserve an (8–) set of copy negatives for eventual use.

Table VII Assembly drawings, component drawings and schedules listed as they would appear in the drawing register

Drawing number	Scale	Title	Comments
A (21) 001–020	1 : 5	External wall details	Assembly details illustrating the entire range of different external wall conditions to be found on the project, including door and window heads and cills, and, in this instance, the footings and ground floor junctions. It would have been equally possible to code these latter conditions A (16)—Foundations, or A (23)—Floors, but these were only two variants on this particular project and common sense prompted their inclusion in the A (21) series rather than a pointless further extension of the elementalisation.
A (27) 001–003 A (27) 501	1 : 5 1 : 5	Eaves details Parapet detail	Parapet and eaves details, however, are covered separately under an A (27)—Roof series, largely because the office possessed a standard parapet assembly drawing which it wished to use on this project, and which was already coded as A (27). It is numbered 501 because it is desirable to keep the sequence of standard drawing numbers well clear of numbers used for specific project purposes. The gaps in numbers which thus appear may be criticised as leading to confusion and doubts on site as to whether they are in possession of the complete set. It is felt, however, that the advantages outweigh these possible objections, and that the objections themselves largely disappear if the drawing register procedures discussed elsewhere are adopted.
A (31) 001–010 A (31) 011–018	1 : 5 1 : 5	External wall opening assemblies—Sheet 1 External wall opening assemblies—Sheet 2	The A (21) series will have covered a number of assemblies which also convey information about secondary elements—eg a lot of the head and cill conditions for windows and external doors. The process of filling in external openings schedules in the format recommended previously will automatically throw up a number of conditions not taken care of in this series and these, together with the jamb conditions, form the subject of the A (31) assemblies.
A (32) 001–006 A (32) 007–012	1 : 5 1 : 5	Internal wall opening assemblies—Sheet 1 Internal wall opening assemblies—Sheet 2	A similar series covering internal openings. Two A1 sheets have been assumed, but the details might equally well have been carried out on a larger number of A4 or A3 sheets. Note that this series conveys assembly information only about the openings themselves—head, jambs and cills where appropriate. Information about what goes in the openings—eg internal door-sets—is given elsewhere in a series of C (32) component drawings. Here again, the necessity for a particular detail will be made apparent by the openings schedule.
A (35) 001–004	1 : 5	Suspended ceiling assemblies	Manufacturers' drawings will often be sufficient for describing the fixing of suspended ceilings. In the present case the drawing covered the timber framework for bulkheads at changes in the ceiling level.
A (37) 001–003	1 : 5	Rooflight assemblies	With the limited elementalisation applied to this set, it may be argued that this drawing could have been grouped under (27)—Roofs, a category which already exists for other purposes.

Table VII (continued)

Component and Sub-component drawings*

Drawing number	Scale	Title	Comments
C (31) 001 to C (31) 008	1 : 20 / 1 : 20	External openings component 1 to External openings component 8	The windows and external doors in this set are conveyed on separate sheets, each sheet giving a dimensioned elevation of what is required. They are supplemented by an SC (31) series of details showing constructional details of the components themselves (timber sections, throatings, fixing of glazing beads, etc).
SC (31) 301–304	1 : 5	Sub-component construction details—sheet 1	As with the assemblies, where a 500 series was used to keep standard drawings separate from the project numbering sequence, here the 300 series is used for a similar purpose.
SC (31) 305–308	1 : 5	Sub-component construction details—sheet 2	
SC (31) 309–312	1 : 5	Sub-component construction details—sheet 3	
C (32) 001 to C (32) 015	1 : 20 / 1 : 20	Internal openings component 1 to Internal openings component 15	Components filling internal openings covered by a similar method. The component is regarded as the door-set, rather than the door. This is in line with modern joinery shop practice and avoids the difficulties of some joinery drawing methods where the door and its frame are treated as separately detailed items, giving rise to problems of co-ordination and of dimensional tolerances. In the present method these problems are placed where they rightly belong, with the manufacturer.
SC (32) 501–504	1 : 5	Sub-component construction details—sheet 1	The component construction details are in a 500 series, being office standard drawings. This is an area that lends itself profitably to standardisation. The overall size of component is specific to the project, but the frame sections are standard regardless of component size.
SC (32) 505–508	1 : 5	Sub-component construction details—sheet 2	
SC (32) 509–512	1 : 5	Sub-component construction details—sheet 3	
SC (32) 513–516	1 : 5	Sub-component construction details—sheet 4	

Schedules

Schedule number	Title	Comments
S (31) 001	Schedule of external openings	When the number of components in a category is small, and/or the number of ways in which potentially they may vary is also small, then it may be left to the appropriate location drawing to identify them, and to the appropriate component drawing to illustrate them. Once you start getting half-a-dozen types, however, and each type may vary as regards its head and jamb assembly, ironmongery and architrave, then it becomes a better bet to number the components on the plan and to refer the searcher to a schedule in which can be tabulated all the variables applying to a given component.
S (31) 101	Schedule of external ironmongery	
S (32) 001	Schedule of internal openings	
S (32) 101	Schedule of internal ironmongery	
S (32) 001	Schedule of manholes	The three main schedules in this set are of this kind. Each gives a numbered list of manholes and openings and uses this as the starting point from which to refer to drawings covering all the variables affecting the component. The ironmongery schedules are rather different in purpose and in format. They are essentially vocabularies of fittings, made up into sets. The opening schedules call up the set of fittings to be fixed to the relevant door or window.

* The examples given are sufficient to illustrate the principle. In practice, other component drawings might cover, for example: copings, pre-cast cladding panels (21), stairs, cat-ladders (24), lintols (31) and (32), balustrades (34), rooflights (37), skirtings (42) litter bins and bollards (70).

This enables drawings to be issued for information only without fear that, for example, the quantity surveyor will measure from an incomplete drawing, or that the contractor will build from unauthorised information.

The method is also of value when a drawing is prepared as a basis for a manufacturer to prepare his own component drawing. In this case the architect prepares his own reference drawing with a status E. This is issued to the manufacturer, whose own working drawing is issued to site, the architect's drawing remaining at status E.

A typical drawing number, containing all the information referred to above, would be as shown in **4.10**.

Circulation
The greater the use that is made of the drawing register the more important does it become to exercise proper discipline in its maintenance and circulation. In particular, it is a useful procedure for the up-dated register (and those of the other consultants) to be copied to all concerned at regular intervals—eg on the first of each month, or as part of the site meeting agenda—so that all team members are aware of the up-to-date position. This is of even greater importance when drawings are being issued in sequence, whether for billing or construction purposes. The recipient's attitude to a given drawing will be conditioned by his knowledge that further amplifying details are envisaged as part of the complete set.

Other people's drawings
The proper recording and storage of incoming drawings often presents a problem, particularly when their numbering system bears no relation to the structure of the architect's own set. Should one open up an incoming drawings register for each consultant and manufacturer, laboriously entering drawing titles and number and date of receipt? Should one even attempt to give each incoming drawing a fresh number, to bring it into line with internal systems, and to aid storage and subsequent retrieval?

These methods are laborious and irksome, and unless they are carried through 100 per cent efficiently they are liable to break down. If only one drawing goes unrecorded because it was needed urgently for reference purposes at the drawing board before anyone had time to enter it in the register, the system collapses, and might as well have never been started.

It is far better to insist on all consultants preparing and circulating their own drawing register in the way previously described. Each office then has a document against which incoming issues may be checked, and by means of which possible omissions and out-of-date revisions may be noted.

As for the storage of incoming drawings, they may be dealt with in the same way as one's own negatives and stored in drawers or hung vertically. Alternatively, they may be folded into A4 size with the drawing number and title outermost, and stored upright on shelves in numerical order. This is simple and space-saving, but presupposes that a drawing register is available in which the search for the required drawing may be initiated.

Issuing drawings
It has already been noted that the drawing register is not a convenient document for recording the issue of drawings to others. Neither, although it is sometimes used for this purpose, is the drawing itself. Indeed, one should perhaps start by questioning the need for such a record in the first place. That drawings, both on completion and on subsequent revision, should go to the people who need them, is perhaps self-evident. Yet instances abound of site staff working from out-of-date information, of revision B going to the structural engineer but not the M & E consultant, of the quantity surveyor being unaware of the expensive revised detail agreed on site and hastily confirmed by a sketch to the contractor but not to him. The fundamental question for anyone engaged in preparing working drawings—Who am I doing this for?—needs to be asked yet again here. Whoever it is being drawn for needs it, and the common-sense procedure of mentally running through the list of everybody whose understanding of the job is remotely changed by the preparation of the new drawing or revision is a valuable discipline for reducing communication gaps. Send to too many rather than to too few is a good maxim.

The keeping of a drawings issue register, however, will not of itself guarantee that the right people get the right drawings. The best we can achieve is to set up disciplines which, if they cannot prevent errors and omissions, can at least assist their detection in due time.

Two such disciplines may be mentioned. First, the use of a drawings issue slip when any drawing leaves the office—even though accompanied by a covering letter—provides an easily leafed-through file record in the issuing drawing office (**4.11**).

Secondly, the routine issue at regular intervals to all members of the team—contractors, sub-contractors and consultants alike—of the drawing register at least enables the recipient to check that he is working to the latest revision of a given drawing, and to some extent throws the onus on him for ensuring that his information is up-to-date.

As to the more mundane question of physically conveying a package of drawings from one office to

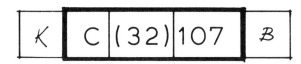

4.10 *A full drawing number, using the system described. The number within the heavy box is the drawing's unique identification and is the minimum information required by anyone searching for it. It indicates that the drawing is of a 'component' filling an 'internal opening', and that it is number '107' in the series. The K at the left indicates that the drawing has been released for construction purposes.*
The issue is Revision B

another, then the larger drawings, unless they are rolled (irritating for the recipient, this), will be folded down to A4 or A3, depending on their volume, and always, of course, with the title panel on the outside. (See **3.21** and **3.22**).

Small drawings, whether of A4 or A3 format, should not be issued loose when they form a set. Their use is sometimes criticised, especially by builders, but a lot of this criticism stems from their misuse in practice rather than from any inherent defect in their size. They are only difficult to co-ordinate if no logical search pattern holds the set together, and they only get out of sequence and get lost if they are issued unbound. It is important therefore that sets of small drawings should be treated as instruction manuals rather than individual sheets, and should be held together accordingly in simple loose-leaf folders. It is anomalous that the motor engineer assembling a car in the protected conditions of a factory or workshop should be given a book of instructions to work from, while the building operative working on precarious scaffolding and battling against wind and rain should traditionally be expected to work from loose sheets of paper flapping round him.

It is appropriate that such bound manuals should contain the drawing register, and some form of guide to the drawing method.

Drawings guide
It is no use preparing your drawings on a well structured and carefully thought out basis if you are the only one who knows about it. Until such time as a standard drawing method becomes universally employed and recognised throughout the building industry, and we are a long way from that, it is incumbent on the producing office to give clear directions as to how its drawings may best be used.

Instruction must take two forms if it is to be effective. There must be a verbal explanation of the method, when the building team is shown the search pattern for information. The initial site meeting is a useful venue

4.11 *Drawings issue form accompanying* all *drawings issued provides a convenient file record of such issues*

for this. There must also be a written guide for subsequent reference, and this will be a useful document to bind into the office manual. Newcomers to the office need to know how the office method works.

An office manual which embodies the drawing and coding methods advocated in this handbook could be prepared for use by members of the office, other consultants and contractors alike. It might be set out as shown below.

Other consultants' drawings
Little has been said so far about the drawings of other consultants and it may be appropriate to comment here on the problems of liaison and co-ordination of drawings produced outside the architect's immediate control. Part of the difficulty arises from the fact that neither the structural engineer nor his M & E counterpart really produces production drawings in the strict sense of the term as it has been used here, ie as a definitive instruction to the builder. Each produces traditionally what is in effect a design drawing, relying on others to provide supplementary information for construction purposes. For example, the structural engineer constantly relies on the architect's drawings to convey such fundamental information as chases in upstand beams for asphalt, throatings in soffits, and the required finish for exposed *in situ* concrete. The M & E consultant is more often than not unable to provide information on, for example, holding down bolts, because the position of these is dependent upon a plant

A guide to these drawings
The drawings in this project have been arranged in the following manner:

1.0 All information in the drawing set is divided into five basic categories of drawing. These are:
- *Location* drawing (coded L) showing *where* anything is—eg where a particular window is located in the building.
- *Component* drawing (coded C) showing *what* it is—eg what the window looks like, how big, etc.
- *Assembly* drawing (coded A) showing *how* it is incorporated in the building—eg how the window relates to the lintol and the cill, and to the wall in which it is built.
- *Sub-component* drawing (coded SC) showing the detailed construction of each component—eg the section of the window frame.
- *Information* drawing (coded IN) giving supplementary information which is relevant, but not part of the building—eg survey drawings, bore hole analyses, etc.

2.0 Each category is then divided into broad sections or elements, each of which deals with a particular work stage. The codes for these are given in brackets following the drawing category, as follows:

(1–)	Substructure	
(2–)	Primary elements	(ie walls, floors, roofs, stairs, frames)
(3–)	Secondary elements	(ie everything filling openings in walls, floors and roofs, suspended ceilings and balustrades)
(4–)	Finishes	
(5–)	Services	
(6–)	Installations	
(7–)	Fixtures	(ie sanitary fittings, cupboards, shelving, etc)
(8–)	Loose equipment	(ie fire extinguishers, unfixed furniture, etc)
(– –)	The project in general	(ie information of a general nature which cannot readily be allocated to any of the other elements).

3.0 All of these codes will not necessarily be used on any project. A list of the elements into which the present set is divided is given at the end of this guide. The element will always be recognisable from the drawing number box however. For example:

L(2–)003 is a location drawing and deals with the positioning and referencing of primary elements. It is the third drawing in that series.

C(3–)012 is a component drawing, and is of a secondary element component, such as a door, or a rooflight. It is the twelfth drawing in that series.

4.0 One further sub-division is built into the system. C(3–) indicates that the drawing deals with a secondary element component. C(32), however, indicates that it is a secondary component in an internal wall, and C(37) that it is a secondary element in a roof. A complete table (known as CI/SfB table I) is given below. Once again all these sub-divisions will not necessarily appear in this drawing set. Furthermore you may well find a location drawing coded L(3–) covering all secondary elements, but containing on it references to component drawings C(31), C(32), C(37), etc. This is so that component drawings relating to windows, internal doors and rooflights respectively may be grouped together for easy reference.

Drawing category	Code	Information conveyed
Location	L	General arrangement plans and elevations, locating all major building elements (walls, doors, windows, etc) and indicating where more detailed information may be found.
Component	C	Showing the size and appearance of all components (eg windows, doors, shutters, fitments, cupboards, etc).
Assembly	A	Demonstrating the manner in which the various building elements and components fit together. Storey sections through external walls are an obvious instance.
Schedule	S	Providing an index to the retrieval of information from other sources.
Sub-component	SC	Showing the manner in which a component is made, eg a timber window would be treated as a component, but sections of the frame, glazing, beads, etc would be the subject of an 'SC' drawing.
Information	IN	Giving background information to the project—survey information, bore holes, pictorials, drawing schedules, etc.

manufacturer who may not have been selected at the time he considered his drawing effort complete. So 'See architect's detail' appears on the structural engineer's drawing (if we are lucky) and 'See manufacturer's shop drawing for setting out of pockets' is frequently the best that can be achieved by M & E. Neither is very satisfactory yet the difficulties in effecting an improvement are substantial, for both spring from an historical and artificial fragmentation of the building process; in the first instance a fragmentation of professional disciplines, in the second an unnatural alienation of the designer and the constructor.

Changing roles
Changing the roles of the profession and the industry may well be desirable, but it is a long-term process and not the function of this book. The best must be made of the present situation. It is therefore incumbent on the architect to acknowledge his management function as co-ordinator of the professional team, and he must accept responsibility for ensuring that the structural engineer is aware of M & E requirements, and that M & E are equally aware of structural constraints. In an imperfect world nobody else is going to do this.

Elemental drawings
Another consideration must be that if we are dealing, as is proposed, with a largely elemental set of drawings as an aid to communication between designer and operative, then it ought to be made possible for a carpenter to build his formwork from the structural engineer's drawings alone, without the need to refer to drawings prepared by others for information which may be vital to him.

Requirement of a formal meeting
It is well for drawings to be prepared by other consultants to be agreed at a formal meeting, which can be minuted, and clearly the architect is in a better position if he has firm proposals and methods worked out to put to the meeting than if he throws the meeting open to suggestions from all sides.

Design team meeting
Such a meeting should cover the following points:

1. *Introductions* Individuals in each organisation must be named as the link men through whom information is to be channelled. They should be of sufficient standing to be able to act and make decisions responsibly and with authority and, if possible, they should be of comparable seniority within their own organisations. It is unhelpful to the project for a young project architect to be out-gunned by the senior partner of the structural engineering consultants.

2. *Procedures* The means by which all team members are to be kept informed must be established. There is no necessity for the architect to insist on acting as a post office, nor need he insist on being party to day-to-day discussions between other consultants, but it is vital that he be kept informed of the outcome of such discussions and that all drawing exchanges are copied to him.

3. *Programme* An example of a programme for the design team has been given in **4.6**. Table it, but do not insist unreasonably on its detailed initial acceptance by other team members against their better judgement. It must at all costs be realistic. But once it has been accepted, it must be taken seriously. Tongue-in-cheek agreement with one eye on an escape route when the inevitable problems occur can be a costly business for everyone.

4. *Format* Thought should have been given at the design stage of the project to the question of suitable production drawing scales and sizes, so the architect should be well prepared to table his proposals for the format. Consistency between all drawing-producing offices is important. Apart from the demonstrable advantages of enabling copy negatives of the architect's basic drawings to be used by other consultants and the reduction of storage and retrieval problems on site, the indefinable air of authority generated by a well organised set of drawings and the impression given of a team well in control of affairs all help in promoting confidence in the team among both outsiders and its own members.

5. *Coding of drawings* It is not essential for all consultants to follow the structuring and coding disciplines that the architect imposes on himself, but nevertheless it is highly desirable that they should be persuaded to do so. In practice it should not be very onerous. All disciplines have their equivalent of the location drawing and all use schedules. These are worth bringing into the structuring method, even though the structural engineer may still adopt his traditional practice of inserting larger scale sections on his general arrangement drawings. If CI/SfB is in use then blanket codes of (16) Foundations and (28) Frame for structural drawings and of (5–) Services and (6–) Installations for services engineers' drawings provide a simple expedient for bringing all disciplines within a common retrieval framework without launching others on to waters the depth of which the architect himself may not yet have plumbed fully.

6. *Definition of responsibilities* Many defects, both of omission and of overlapping information, may be avoided if the responsibilities of each team member can be defined precisely at the outset of the project. Apart from the more straightforward contractual responsibilities which it is assumed will have been covered in the respective letters of appointment but which it will be sensible to confirm at this inaugural meeting (matters such as, for example, who tackles lifts, cold water supply, drainage, roads and footpaths; who details and checks pre-cast concrete components, etc) there are grey areas where some early agreement will be of benefit. The allocation to the structural drawing office of the responsibility for indicating accurately detailed profiles has already been referred to. Reinforced concrete staircases provide another area where it is unnecessary and confusing for the architect to prepare elaborately detailed sections for the benefit of a contractor who is going to build from the structural engineer's drawings anyway. An early agreement should be reached to limit the architect's role to providing

design profiles within which the structural engineer may work, and against which the structural details may be checked subsequently.

Drawing office programming

The design team programme will have identified the time available for production of the working drawings, and the first shot at the drawing register will have revealed the magnitude of the task. The reconciliation of one with the other, and of both with the financial resources available, is one of the essential arts of architectural management, and as such demands more space than can be devoted to it in the present handbook. Certain points may usefully be made however.

Size of drawing office team

The right size and structure of the team is all-important, and in many ways it is a case of the smaller the better. Any increase over a team of one starts to invoke the law of diminishing returns and as the numbers increase so do the problems of control and communications. On the other hand, the diversity of work demanded by most building projects coupled with the constant and remorseless pressures of the overall programme mean that too small a team lacks the necessary flexibility of response.

In practical terms, the size of the team will be the size of the task in man-weeks divided by the number of weeks available, and if the latter is unreasonably low then the team becomes unwieldy and difficult to co-ordinate. In any case, the size of the team is bound to fluctuate throughout the working drawing period, with a small but high-powered element at stage E, rising to a peak soon after commencement of stage F, and tailing off towards the end of that stage as the main flow of information to the quantity surveyor is completed (**4.12**).

Production drawing programme

The production drawings, if properly structured so that a predetermined amount of information is conveyed in them, should be the simplest aspect of the architect's work to quantify in terms of time taken. Having established the list of drawings, it is better for two of the more experienced people to make independent assessments of the time that should be taken over each drawing and to compare notes afterwards. Factors of personal optimism or pessimism may thus be discounted, and a more realistic time allocation made. But experience is everything, and an inquest after the programme has been completed, with feedback of the actual time taken over each drawing as against the time budgeted for, is essential if future programmes are to be timed more accurately.

Priorities

In framing the stage F programme certain priorities will emerge. Clearly the establishment of the basic set of location plan negatives is fundamental, for they will form the basis for elementalisation of subsequent location plans and of other consultants' work. After that the priorities will probably be dictated by the needs of the quantity surveyor. An elemental format makes it easier to group the issue of drawings into separate packages—eg internal joinery, finishes, etc, but this is only helpful if the packages are genuinely complete. Few quantity surveyors will object to receiving information piecemeal, but an early issue of the openings schedule, with half the details it refers to still incomplete, only leads to an abortive start being made on the measurement. On the other hand, the fact that drawings of the basic structure may be issued and measured without having to wait for the finishes to be added to the same sheet does allow a bigger overlap of the production drawings and billing programmes.

Drawings should be allocated to team members in the form of a simple bar chart. By this means, everyone can see his personal short-term and long-term targets, and a competitive element may be introduced (**4.13**).

Introducing new methods

The introduction of structured drawings into an office which hitherto has managed without them requires some thought. There must be many offices which, whilst agreeing in principle that their work could be improved by rationalisation of their working drawing methods, are reluctant to take the first step on what might prove to be a seductively attractive slippery slope.

As with dieting and daily exercising the two important things are to start today rather than tomorrow and not to be put off by the prophecies of failure which will be made by those around you. In this latter respect, one common fallacy may be dispelled at the outset. You will

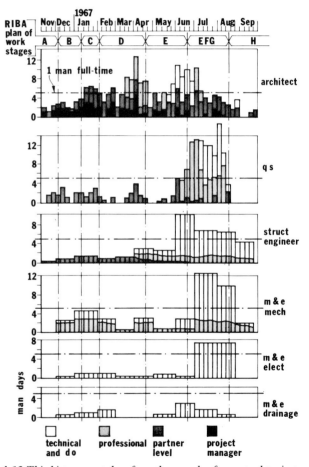

4.12 *This histogram, taken from the records of an actual project, shows the difficulties of co-ordinating multi-disciplinary efforts. The peaking of resources during the production drawing stage is clearly shown*

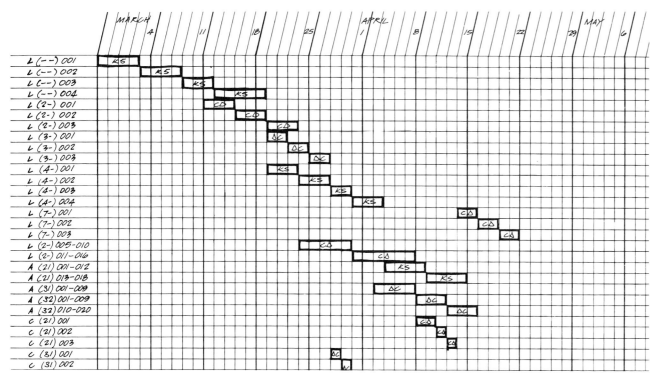

4.13 *A drawing office programme allocates individual team members appropriate work loads. The elemental approach means that DC, for example, can follow the (3-) element right through, dealing with it in its location, component and assembly aspects*

be told confidently that architects are individualists and will fight tooth and nail against any suggestion of rationalised drawing, standardised detailing or mathematically oriented coding systems. This you will find to be untrue, architects being as fundamentally lazy and anxious for a trouble-free existence as anyone else. Experience indicates that given a commonsense system which is fundamentally easy to use, people will use it.

The sequence to take
But take one step at a time. There are several degrees of rationalisation and they should be introduced in sequence:
• Standardise drawing size and format for all new projects entering production drawing stage.
• Rationalise new projects into the schedule, location, assembly, component format.
• Select one such project for the experimental application of CI/SfB coding and let it run through its production phase before attempting a general application of the method. You will thus have built up some office case-law to assist in answering the query 'How do we code for this situation?' which will arise on subsequent projects.
• Now that you have each project producing component and assembly information in a common format and within the context of a coding system offering ease of retrieval, you are in a position, if you so wish, to introduce standard solutions to various aspects of your detailing.

What does it cost?
As to the cost of introducing (and indeed of operating) new drawing methods one is on less certain ground.

WORKING DRAWING MANAGEMENT

Certainly all the available feedback suggests that it is unusual for a practice to revert to unstructured working drawings once it has started producing structured sets, which seems to indicate that at least the structured set is not so overwhelmingly expensive to produce as to render it uneconomic in practice. Short of carrying out parallel drawing exercises using two methods and comparing the cost there is no real way of being sure.

What is clear, however, is that the more comprehensive nature of the information likely to be produced within a structured format, its greater potential for co-ordination and the greater ease of information retrieval which it offers to the contractor, will all combine to reduce time-consuming queries once the work is on site. An honest analysis of office time spent on so-called 'site operations' is perhaps a salutary exercise for any practice. Bearing in mind that the plan of work defines this stage as consisting of 'Following plans through to practical completion of the building', consider how much time in practice is spent in the drawing office in amending existing drawings and in providing new ones to illustrate details which could (and in retrospect clearly should) have been provided during the working drawings stage. Consider also the predictable reaction of the poor unfortunate who is dragged back a year later from the multi-million pounds Arabian Nights fantasy on which he is happily engaged in order to sort out the door detail he had unfortunately omitted from the working drawing set which had been his previous task. (In Parkinsonian terms it may be stated that if x is the time spent in hoping the problem will just go away, y is the time spent in reconciling oneself to the fact that it isn't going to, z is the time spent in seeking out the necessary reference documents, and t is the amount of drawing time the detail should reasonably take, then the sum of $x + y + z$ will be inversely proportional to t. But never less than a week.) It must always be cheaper to produce information at the right time. On the other hand, any change in working method must have some cost implication, as the change to metric dimensioning demonstrated. As with metrication, this cost should be looked upon as an investment for the future.

5
Other methods

Towards the future
The 1972 Report on Structuring Project Information had this to say about building communications:
'if today's best practice in the traditional presentation of information could become the norm within the next five years, this would effect an immediate improvement in the performance of the industry as a whole . . .'

The present book has been an attempt to identify and to describe this 'best practice', and since this seemed to be a sufficient task in itself little attention has been given to methods and developments which appeared to go beyond the mainstream of current practice, and to belong more to the future than to the present. We must now, in this final chapter, take a brief look at some of them. This is necessary not only because today's *avant-garde* innovation is likely to become tomorrow's accepted practice, but because we need to reassure ourselves that the principles set out in this book are fundamental enough, and the methods advocated flexible enough, to accommodate changing requirements without the necessity for drastic re-structuring.

Conversion, alteration and rehabilitation
To suggest that work coming under this heading is outside the mainstream of normal practice, or that techniques for dealing with it are in any way *avant-garde* is, of course, a misnomer. Such projects have always formed the mainstay of many smaller practices, and there is an increasing tendency for building owners to look towards adaptation of existing premises rather than building new.

They have been included in this final section because in order to outline the principles of working drawing production simply it was thought desirable to limit the field under consideration, and up to now all the examples shown have been of drawings for new buildings. It is now necessary to look at the methods described previously, and to see how far they are applicable to the description of work to existing buildings.

To dispose of the simple matters first, straightforward extensions to buildings present no problem. They are in every respect new pieces of building and there is no reason why the methods adopted for any other new building, and the conditions relating to their use, should not apply.

Where information needs to be given about work to existing structures two additional aspects need consideration which are not present in entirely new work. One is the question of demolitions, particularly demolitions within a structure. The other is the question of repairing and making good.

Whenever any demolition of existing structures is involved, no matter how modest, it is preferable to show it on a separate drawing— to regard it, in fact, as one more element in the elementalised set. The expression 'demolition' is to be interpreted widely in this connection, including such items as forming an opening in an existing wall as well as more major demolitions involving entire sections of the building. The correct way to deal with an opening to be cut in an existing brick wall to take a new door and frame is shown in **5.1** The drawing deals with the forming of the opening as a single activity, including the insertion of the new lintol over. It could hardly be dealt with otherwise by the builder. The drawing showing the new work (**5.2**) refers only to the new door and frame, inserted in what by then is an existing opening.

Note that it would be wrong for the drawing showing new works to make reference to the opening having been formed under the same contract. To do so would be to invite the possibility of the estimator unintentionally including the item twice. Neither is the routine note 'make good to plaster and finishes' included on either drawing. Such a general instruction, which will presumably apply to a number of such door openings throughout the project, is more appropriate to the specification.

Generally speaking, a single demolition plan for each floor will suffice, but if there are complexities of a special nature to be covered then the mode of conveying the information may need to be more elaborate. Figure **5.3**, for example, shows the demolition drawing of a reflected ceiling plan, where the fact that certain suspended ceiling tiles and light fittings were to be removed is carefully separated from the new work which is to replace them, (**5.4**), as well as from the alterations to internal partitions, etc which are covered on another sequence of drawings.

Simple items of making good, such as the replacement of areas of plaster, or the overhauling and repair of windows, are often most simply covered by scheduling on a room to room basis. If only 2m² of plaster are to be replaced in a given room, it is presumably obvious enough to all concerned which 2m² are referred to, without the necessity of precisely locating them on an internal elevation. Written description, in fact, is often better than graphical instruction in much rehabilitation work.

If CI/SfB coding is being adopted for the set then demolition drawings will normally be given a (– –) 'project in general' code, leaving the more detailed code references for application to the new works.

One extremely important point is often overlooked in drawings of alteration work, with unfortunate consequent effects. It is absolutely vital that everyone should be clear from the drawings as to what is new work and what is existing. Basic structure is not too difficult to distinguish (shading in existing walls and showing the details of construction on new walls will avoid confusion in this respect), but it is the little things—manholes, rainwater pipes, sanitary fittings—often appearing as left-overs from the survey drawing, which need specific annotation.

It is, of course, helpful to issue the survey drawing as part of the set.

Activity drawings
The provision of a new door in the existing brick wall given as an example in the section on conversions and alterations was an instance of an activity-oriented approach to the provision of building information. Activity 1, involving the cutting of the opening and insertion of the lintol, was rightly regarded as being distinct and of a different nature from activity 2, which embraced the fixing of a new door and frame. The two activities were separate and complete in themselves; they were potentially capable of being carried out by different people, or groups of people; and they might well have been (and indeed probably were) separated from each other by a significant period of time, during which no work of any kind was being done to either the opening or the door. It was possible, therefore, and on the face of it reasonable, to convey the necessary information to the builder in the form of two separate instructions.

Whilst this approach to building communications is clearly sensible in the very limited context of alteration work, it is also possible to apply it to the whole spectrum of building operations. Hitherto in this book a building has been looked upon as consisting of an assembly of individual elements. It may equally well be regarded as the result of a sequence of different and separately identifiable activities. Such a concept lay

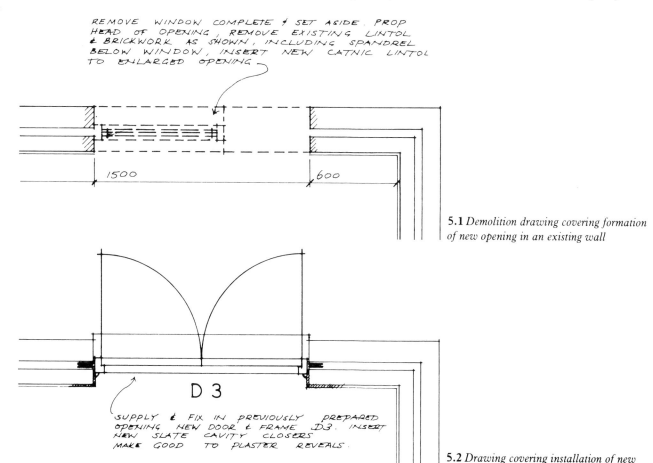

5.1 *Demolition drawing covering formation of new opening in an existing wall*

5.2 *Drawing covering installation of new door and frame in the opening formed in* **5.1**

WORKING DRAWINGS HANDBOOK

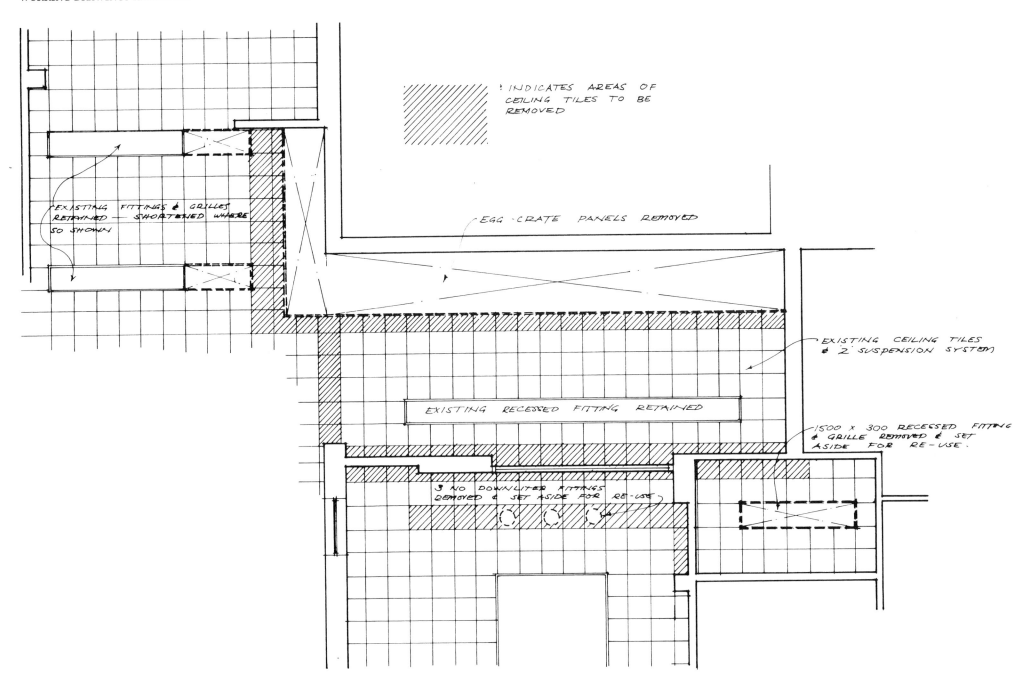

5.3 *Demolition drawing of reflected ceiling plan (scale 1:50)*

OTHER METHODS

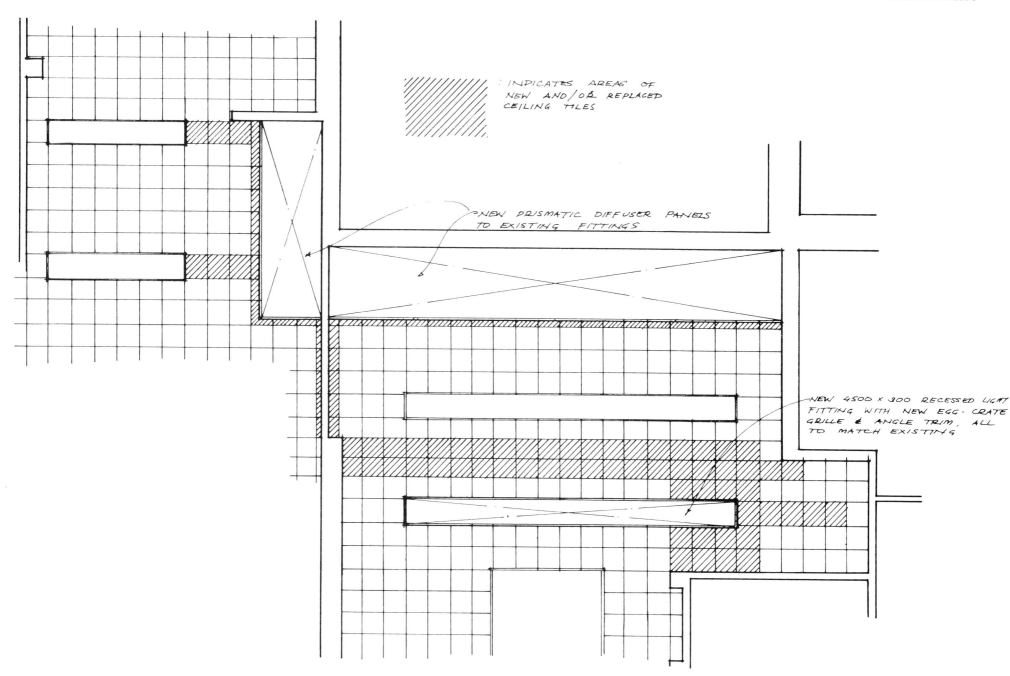

5.4 *Drawing showing new works replacing demolitions shown in* **5.3** *(scale 1:50)*

behind the development in the 1960s of activity and operations bills of quantities. The theory behind them is simple. The contractor's main problem lies in the organisation of his resources, both material and human. His bricks have to arrive on site at the right time, his bricklaying labour force has to be sufficient to optimise the length of time his scaffolding is on hire, it must be re-deployed smoothly and economically when the work is finished, either to some other part of the project, or to another project. Success lies in careful and accurate programming.

Conventional bills of quantities do little to assist in this task. To tell the contractor that he is to erect a total of x m² of brick wall will enable him to put an overall price on the total brickwork/bricklayer section. It will not point out to him that the last brick will be laid some eighteen months after the first; nor that it will be laid on an entirely different part of the site; nor that the nature of the construction involves the total bricklaying operation being split into three separate stints, with substantial gaps of time between them.

Such information may well be deducible from an intelligent examination of the drawings, but the bill of quantities is after all the document he has to price, and were it to be presented in a form which showed the true nature of his work there would be inestimable benefits all round. The contractor would have at his disposal not only a more accurate basis for his estimating, but a flexible management tool which could be used for, among other things, the programming of material deliveries, the deployment of site labour, and the forecasting of cash flow for the project. The quantity surveyor would have the advantage that re-measurement, when necessary, would be restricted to small and readily identifiable sections of the work rather than entire trade sections, and that valuations for interim certificates and final account would be greatly simplified. (It would not be a question of agreeing how many metres of brickwork had, in fact, been erected. It would be a matter of common observation how many activities had been completed.)

The method has not become so widely established as had at one time seemed likely, but it is there, readily available, and consideration should be given as to whether any adjustment of working drawing technique is desirable to accompany it.

The method starts with the establishment of a notional list of building activities which, while not binding on the contractor, is nevertheless intended as a realistic attempt to put the work into a correct order. A typical sequence for a piece of brick walling, for example, might run thus:
1. Strip top soil.
2. Excavate for strip footings.
3. Blind base of excavation.
4. Lay concrete.
5. Lay engineering bricks to DPC level.
6. Lay DPC
7. Build 275 mm cavity wall to wall plate level, etc.

It is not possible for drawings to show activities, only the completed event. There is no reason, however, why an elementalised set of location drawings such as has been discussed in the previous pages should not form a perfectly satisfactory adjunct to an operational bill. In the example given, activities 1 to 4 would all be covered on the foundation plan, and the remaining three on the primary elements plan. To each drawing would be added a note saying which numbered activities were shown on it (or were shown on other drawings to which that drawing referred). Against each activity in the list would be set the number of the location drawing which would initiate the search pattern.

Overlay draughting
Overlay draughting (or pin registration as it is sometimes known in the USA) is a development of the fundamental elementalisation techniques described in chapter 2. As such it differs from other methods more in its approach to production drawing management than in its basic presentation of building information.

Central to the method is the use on all drawing boards of a 'pin bar', consisting of a strip of sprung steel with projecting steel pins set at centres compatible with small holes pre-punched in the drawing sheets. By this means it is possible for a series of different negatives to be located accurately one above the other, and to be moved between drawing boards—and indeed between offices—without loss of precision. When the medium used is a high quality drafting film the degree of transparency is such that a composite process negative, or 'inter-print', may be made from as many as five overlaid negatives. This has a number of implications. Whereas the basic location plan negative described in chapter 2 was designed to be the forerunner of a series of process negatives, each of which was then lined in, added to and annotated to show the work involved in the particular element to be described, overlay draughting allows the basic negative itself to be fragmented into a number of more fundamental negatives (one showing the grid, for example, one showing the structural frame, one showing the walls, etc) (5.5).

Only those aspects of the basic building form which are relevant to a particular element or the work of a

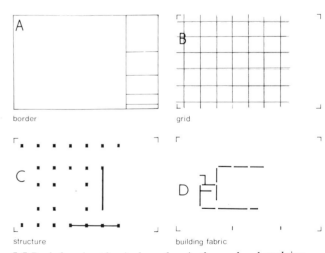

5.5 *Basic location plan is shown here in the overlay draughting method separated into four constituent negatives*

particular consultant need to be used for that particular purpose, affording a greater simplicity in the appearance, and hence in the subsequent interpretation of the elemental drawing.

The way in which other consultants may use the original negatives is illustrated in **5.6** and **5.7**, where combinations of overlays are shown for, respectively, the structural engineer's foundation plan and the services engineer's lighting layout.

Where used on a large project the method offers both the possibilities of substantial cost savings and considerable sophistication in presentation. The illustrations to this section are taken from drawings prepared for a 900-person village in Afghanistan by Yakeley Associates, a project where the very large numbers of prints required from each composite negative (as many as 120 in some instances) led to printing by offset litho from half-size plates made photographically. The fact that the drawings showing elemental information existed separately from, instead of simply added to, the basic negative allowed them to be printed in different colours on the composite print.

Even where colour is not used, the combination of multiple negatives with the offset litho process enables a grey half-tone to be used to suppress the basic non-elemental information on the finished print, while the elemental information which constitutes the real purpose of the drawing is printed in the full black line.

Clearly the use of the overlay method requires that the architect, in his role of co-ordinator for the whole building and consultant team, devote a substantial amount of administrative time to the undertaking. Nevertheless the potential savings in production time and in overheads (printing and postage, for example), and the inherent advantage of having all consultants working from the same base information and producing a uniform set of drawings, make the method a genuine contender whenever a large production drawing programme is under consideration.

Certain matters are vital:
- only a high quality drafting film will give the required dimensional stability and transparency
- a strict procedure must be adopted for dealing with photographers and printers. (The print order form used in the Afghanistan project is shown in **5.8**
- the large number of negatives generated demands an adequate numbering, filing and retrieval method
- where photographic reduction to half-size plates is being used a line thickness of 0.25 mm should be regarded as a minimum for use on the original.

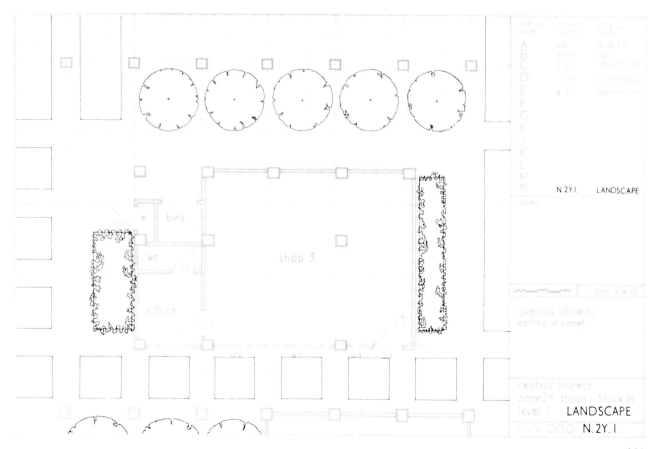

5.6 and **5.7** *Negatives produced by other consultants are added as overlays to selected negatives from the architect's original basic drawings to produce composite interprints*

111

WORKING DRAWINGS HANDBOOK

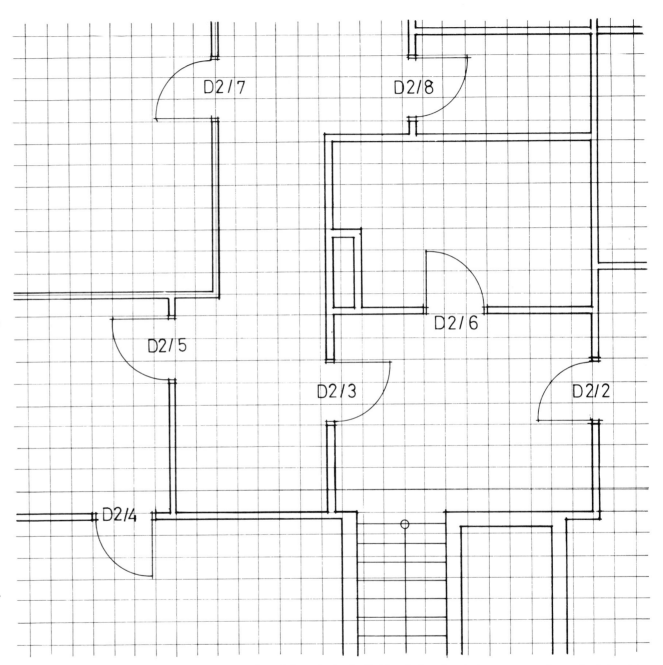

5.8 *Complexities of photographic and printing sequences necessitate proper administrative control, as by this print order form*

Grids

The use of shadow grids has been around for a long time, particularly among the manufacturers of building systems, where components tend to be modular and junctions simple and standardised. They are applicable to traditional building as well however whenever a modular discipline exists, and when used with discretion can speed up the production of drawings and reduce the need for elaborate dimensioning.

Where grids are combined with the use of pre-printed sheets a half-tone is usually adopted for the printing of the grid itself, so that it appears on the finished print in a fainter line than those used for the rest of the drawing. In practical terms, the use of grids is limited to location plans, and they are of greatest benefit in projects where rationalisation of the design has restricted the size and position of the elements. In **5.9**, for example, where the use of a grid of 6 mm squares has allowed each square to represent a 300 mm module at a scale of 1:50, the

5.9 *Modular discipline eliminates the need for complicated dimensioning by limiting the location of elements to certain standard situations (scale of original 1:50)*

112

placing of the 100 mm partition has been limited to one of three conditions. It is either centred on a grid line, centred on a line midway between grid lines, or has one face coinciding with a grid line. Similarly the door-frame, with a co-ordinating dimension of 900 mm, is always situated so that it occupies three entire grids.

No dimensions are needed to locate such elements if the discipline for positioning them is established from the outset and is known to everyone using the drawings.

A word of warning however. It is not realistic to expect the man on site to set out a wall by counting grids and doing his own calculation. Dimensions should always be added to the grid for key setting-out positions, overall lengths, and controlling dimensions.

Computer graphics
Nowhere in the whole field of technological advance is the speed of development, the sheer explosion of information and techniques, so dramatic as in the area of computer applications. The microchip would seem to have had the same liberating effect on the cybernetics industry as the invention of the internal combustion engine once had on mechanical transportation.

Any attempt here to survey the field of computer graphics in detail would be futile; in the first place the subject would need a book to itself, and in the second place what was written would be likely to become out-of-date before it had emerged from the printer. Nevertheless, one or two comments on likely future developments may be usefully made. The computer is here to stay.

The distinction must again be emphasised between the two demands made on the architect engaged in the overall working drawing process—the solution of the technical problem and its subsequent documentation. The ability of the computer to hold and evaluate rapidly an almost infinite range of variables gave an initial impetus to its use in the first of these. Such applications as the optimisation of cut and fill when siting a building

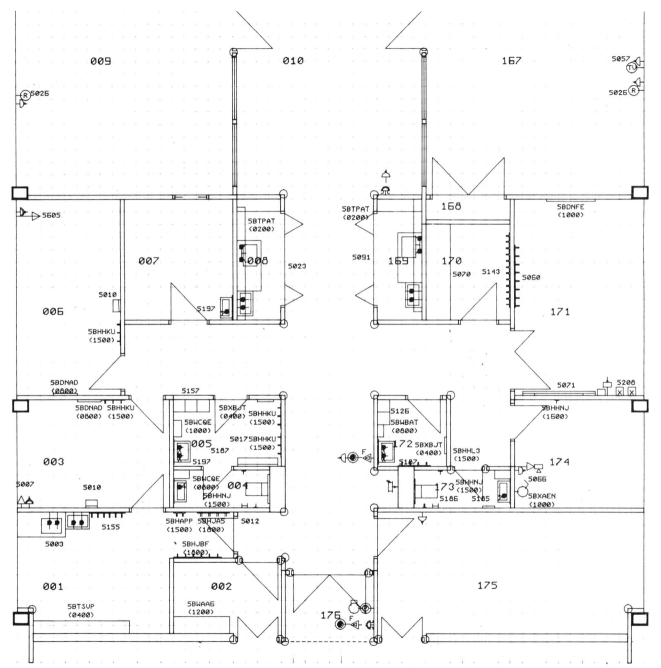

5.10 *Part of a working drawing produced by a digital plotter as part of the DHSS Harness hospitals project. The computer graphics system in this case was linked to an automatic measurement system and bill of quantities production (see p 116)*

WORKING DRAWINGS HANDBOOK

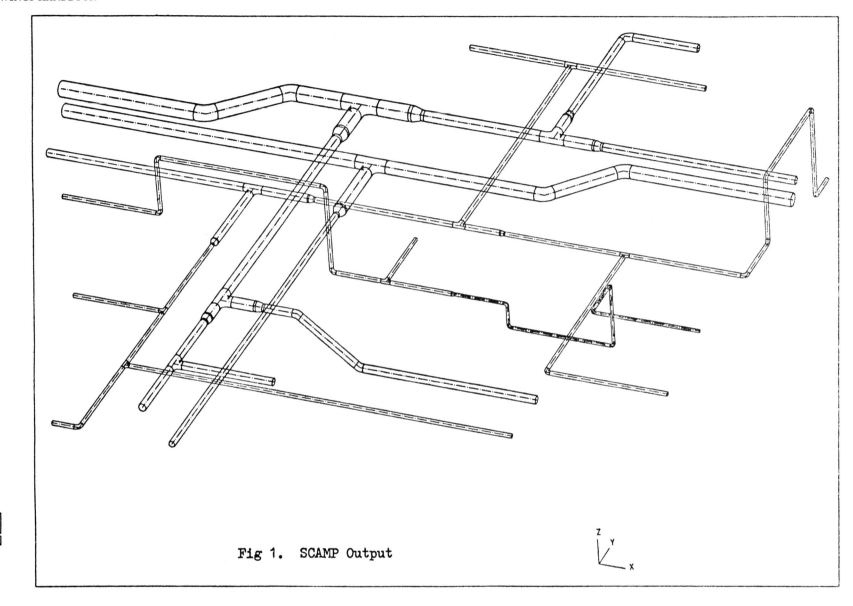

5.11 *Computer not only shows assembly in perspective but has the ability to change the view-point at will*

OTHER METHODS

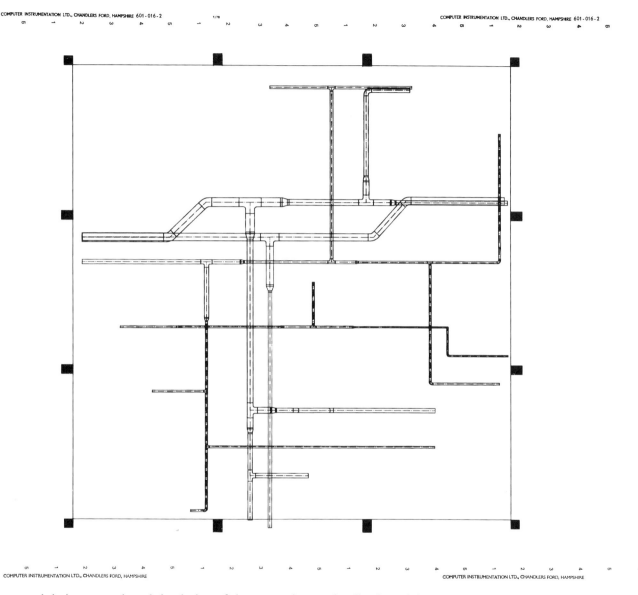

5.12 *(left) Plan view of* **5.11**

5.13 *(above) A typical high resolution graphics work station*

on undulating ground, and the design of the external fabric to meet heat-loss requirements, are now commonplace. The development of further similar applications is at present limited more by the architect's difficulty in identifying his own design processes than by the computer's ability to quantify them for him.

Application of the computer to the secondary process of documenting solutions has until now been inhibited by the expense involved. The existence of a building project, or series of projects, on a sufficiently large scale was necessary before the use of a digital plotter became economically justifiable, but where the right circumstances existed the possibilities were enormous and exciting. The Harness hospital concept, developed by the Department of Health and Social Security, in which the basic data banks and documentation were intended to be available for a programme of some fifty hospitals, involved an inter-active system whereby the substitution of different components in the digitally plotted drawings automatically produced corresponding changes in the schedules, bills of quantities and costings (**5.10**, p 113).

Now a number of things are happening simultaneously, and the consequences cannot yet be foreseen:
• the cost of computer graphics is reducing sharply, opening up the facility to a much wider range of projects than had been economically feasible before
• increasing sophistication in the software and hardware now available opens up possibilities of perspective presentation of information which may well prove to be a better method of communication than the traditional system of plan, elevation, and section developed for manual techniques (**5.11**).

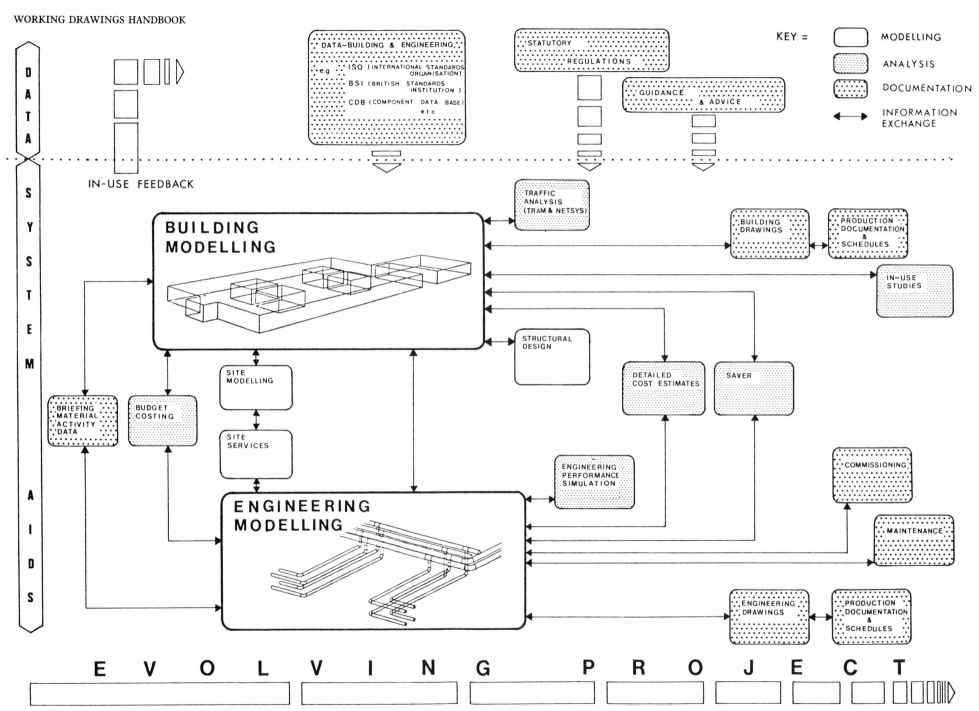

5.14 *DHSS computer applications in total Health Buildings system*

- a situation now arises when the solution to a technical problem may be presented by the computer in a form which is immediately acceptable as the final documentation.

A glance at the range of computer applications developed by the DHSS for its total Health Building System indicates the pervasive influence that computers now have on almost every aspect of architectural practice (**5.14**).

Possibilities such as these must inevitably change a lot of our attitudes to building communications. In the same way that the early modes of computer draughting attempted a mechanical simulation of manual methods, so is it likely that the new computer-produced graphical forms will have an influence on conventional drawings.

Common arrangement
The Co-ordinating Committee for Project Information (CCPI) was set up at the end of 1979, its terms of reference being: '. . . to identify the measures necessary to ensure the preparation of agreed and co-ordinated standard conventions for the production of drawings, specifications and measurement'. Its Stage 2 Report was published for comment at the end of 1984, and final implementation of its recommendations in the form of Codes of Procedure is scheduled for the Autumn of 1986.

The Common Arrangement of Production Information (CA) is an ambitious undertaking, designed to bring greater uniformity into the classification of building information, whether it be drawings, specifications or Bills of Quantities. The entire building process is divided into 24 alphabetically coded 'Work Sections', for example A – Preliminaries/General Conditions, B – Complete Buildings, C – Demolitions/ Alterations/Maintenance, D – Groundwork, etc. Each section is then sub-divided (D – Groundwork, for example, into ten further categories – ground investigation, soil stabilisation, site de-watering, excavation and soil/hand filling, etc) and each sub-division is closely defined to avoid ambiguity.

What effect the Common Arrangement is likely to have on established working methods and systems is not easy to foresee, but in the field of written information at least the provision of specifications and Bills of Quantities using similarly defined work section classifications must have benefits.

The Report is less specific with regard to drawings. The Location/Assembly/Component/Schedule basis for primary structuring of information is endorsed (see p. 4 – The structure of working drawings), but the possibility of secondary structuring by Common Arrangement work sections is discounted, on the grounds that such classification is not appropriate to drawings which, by their very nature, embrace on one sheet of paper a number of work sections. The draft is cautious about both the desirability of secondary structuring for all projects and the best method of achieving it.

As this second edition goes to press the most likely indications are that the Code of Procedure will recommend:
- primary structuring of information into the Location/ Assembly/Component/Schedule format
- classification and annotation of these elements by C1/SfB
- a modification of existing C1/SfB categories, where this is both desirable and possible, to bring them closer into line with CA work section categories.

This would represent a practical compromise with which few in the building industry would quarrel; but the concept of a complete building information system, with every participant at every level knowing precisely the type and quality of information expected of him, and what he in return might expect from others, remains as elusive of achievement as ever.

Appendix 1
Building elements and external features

The degree of detail used in representing any element is dependent on the scale at which it is shown. The examples given below give an indication of what may be considered appropriate for various scales.

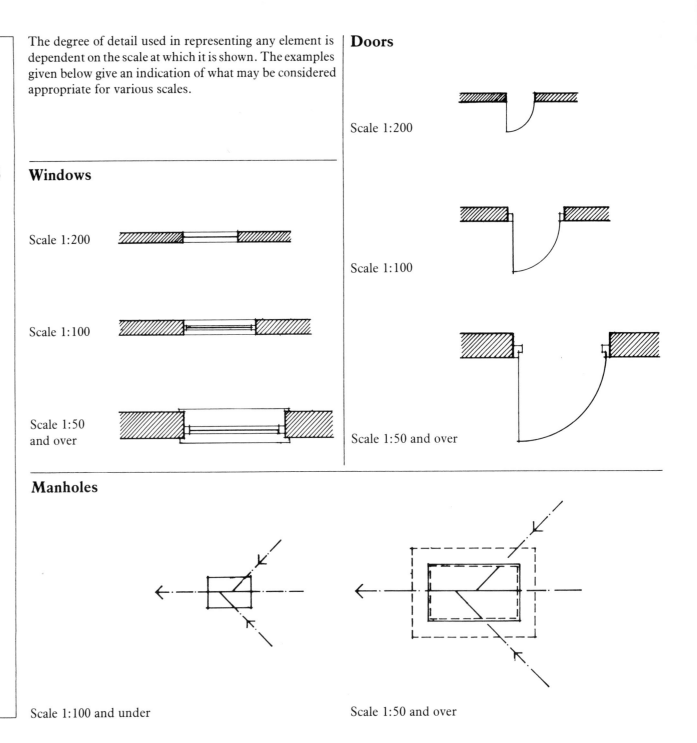

APPENDIX 1

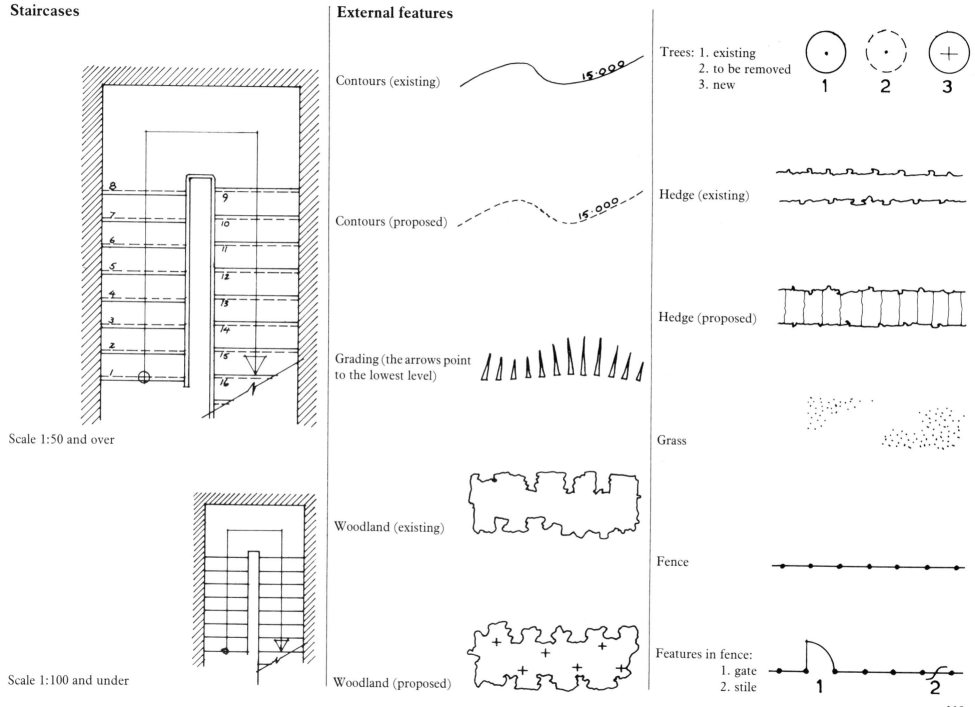

119

Appendix 2
Conventions for doors and windows

Doors

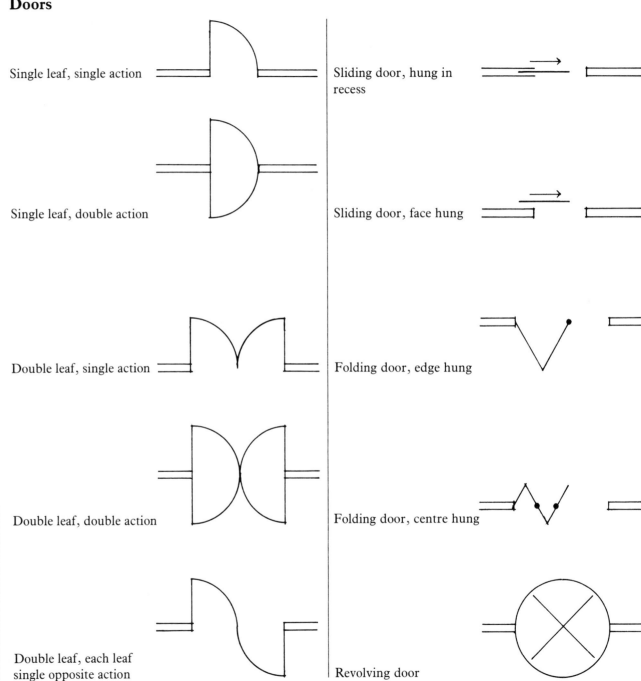

Single leaf, single action

Single leaf, double action

Double leaf, single action

Double leaf, double action

Double leaf, each leaf single opposite action

Sliding door, hung in recess

Sliding door, face hung

Folding door, edge hung

Folding door, centre hung

Revolving door

120

APPENDIX 2

Windows

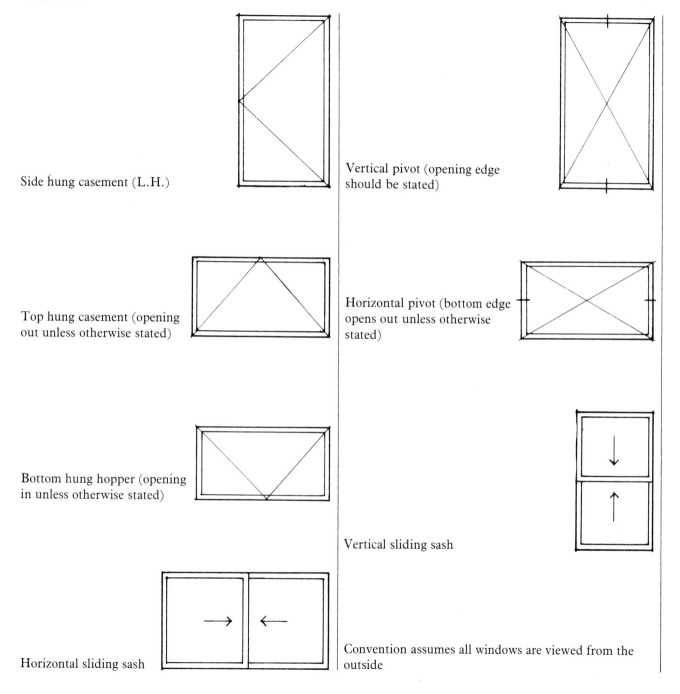

Appendix 3
Symbols indicating materials

Blockwork

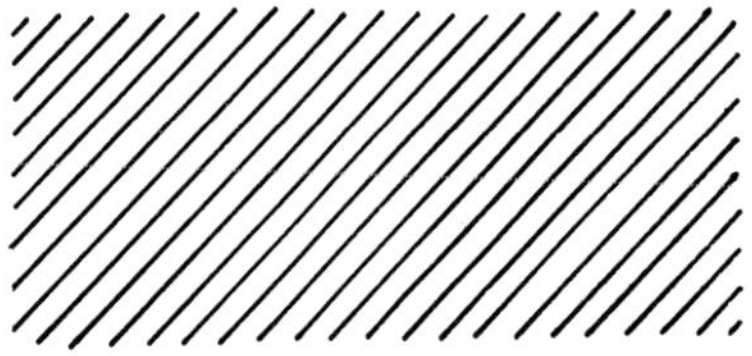

Brickwork

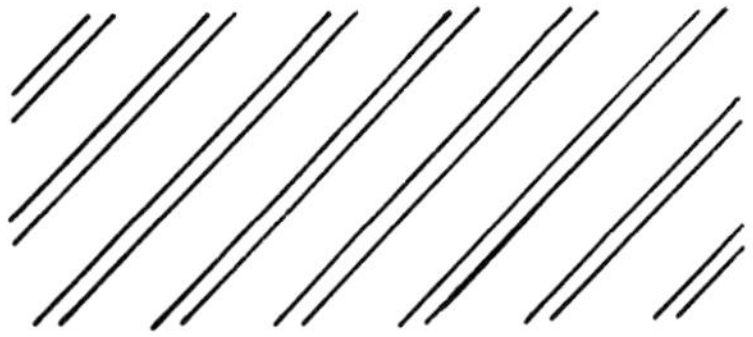

Earth

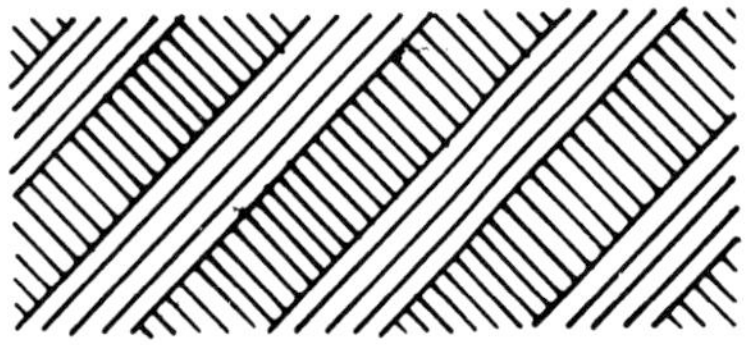

Concrete

Hardcore

Precast concrete

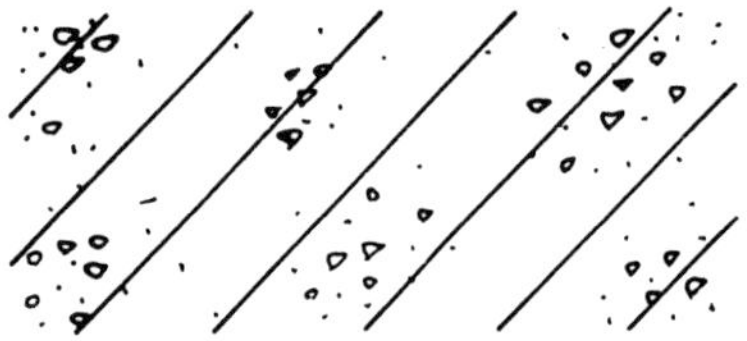

Blockwork (commonly used alternative)

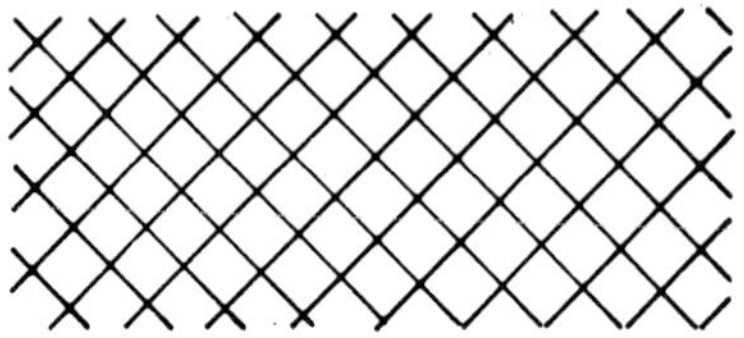

Stone

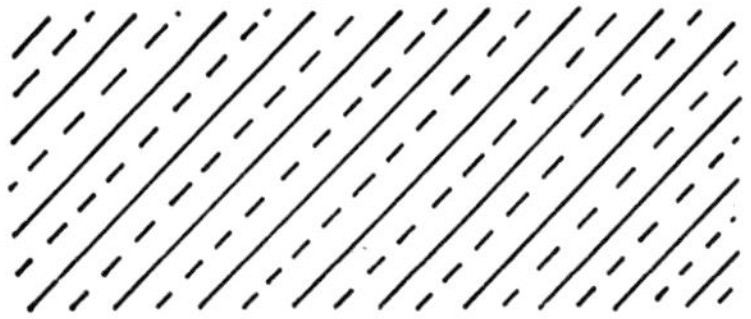

Marble

Rubble stonework

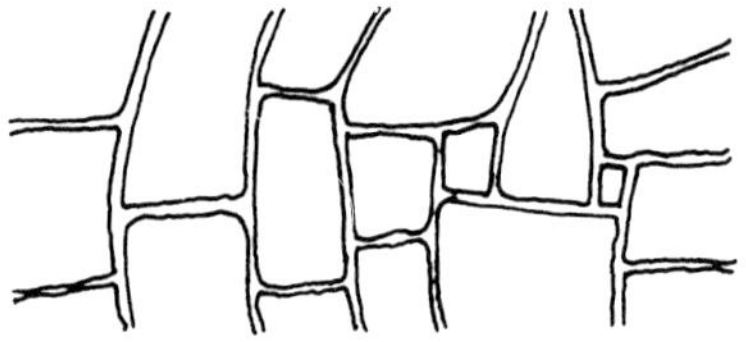

Slate

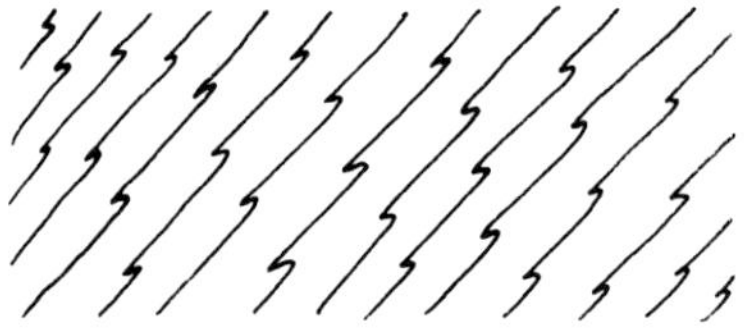

Insulation

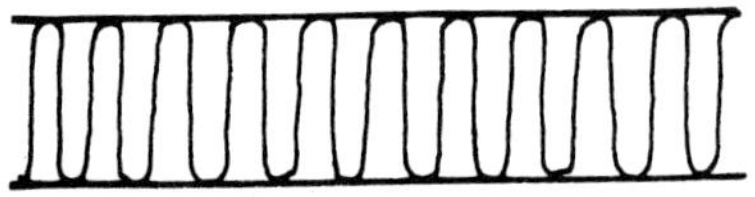

APPENDIX 3

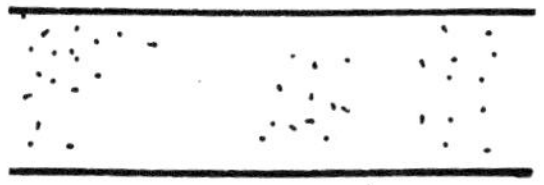

Some abbreviations in common use

alum.	aluminium
asb.	asbestos
bit.	bitumen (or bituminous)
bk.	brick
bkwk.	brickwork
C.I.	cast iron
conc.	concrete
cp.	chromium plated
h/wd.	hardwood
PVA.	polyvinyl acetate
PVC.	polyvinyl chloride
PCC.	pre-cast concrete
rfmt.	reinforcement
SAA.	satin anodised aluminium
SS.	stainless steel
s/wd.	softwood
t & g	tongued and grooved
UPVC.	unplasticised polyvinyl chloride
W.I.	wrought iron

Unwrot timber section

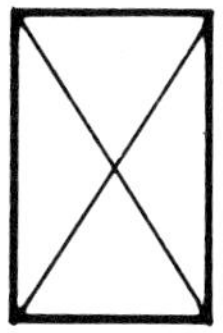

Wrot timber section

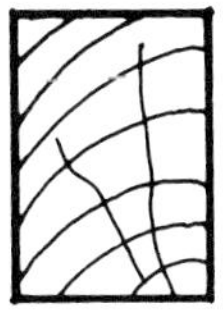

Wrot timber section on two faces

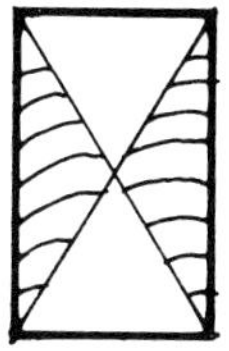

Metal (at large scale)

Metal (at small scale)

Plaster (or cement screed)

Appendix 4
Electrical, telecommunications and fire protection symbols

The symbols for use in these fields are covered in a number of publications, primarily:
BS 1192: 1969 *Recommendations for building drawing practice*
PD 6479: 1976 *Symbols and other conventions for building production drawings*
BS 3939: 1972 *Graphical symbols for electrical power, telecommunications and electrics diagrams*
BS 1635: 1970 *Graphical symbols and abbreviations for fire protection drawings*

The symbols shown here represent a small selection of those available. They have been restricted to those which the architect is most likely to encounter when dealing with the type of small-scale work in which an electrical consultant has not been appointed.

Certain symbols are differently represented in different Standards. Furthermore, other symbols have acquired a use in practice but do not appear in any laid down Standard. In such cases the most common usage has been given.

Reference should be made to the British Standards listed above for more comprehensive lists of symbols.

Main control or intake

Distribution board

Earth

Consumer's earthing terminal

Single pole one way switch

Similar, but the number indicates the number of switches at one point

Two pole one way switch

Cord operated single pole one way switch

Two way switch

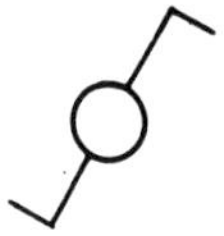

Dimmer switch

Period limiting switch

Time switch

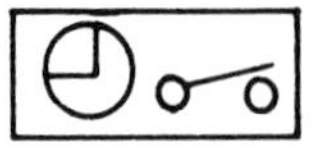

APPENDIX 4

Thermostat	
Push button	
Luminous push button	
Key operated switch	
Socket outlet	
Switched socket outlet	
Double socket outlet	
Lighting point—ceiling mounted	
Emergency lighting point	
Lighting point—wall mounted	
Lighting point with integral switch	
Single fluorescent lamp	
Three fluorescent lamps	
Outdoor lighting standard	
Outdoor lighting bollard	
Illuminated sign	
Illuminated emergency sign	
Electric bell	
Clock (or slave clock)	
Master clock	

125

Telecommunications

Telecommunications socket outlet.
State use—eg TV (for television)
         R (for radio)
         etc.

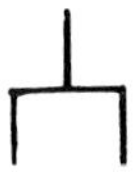

Aerial

Telephone point (to exchange lines)

Telephone point (internal only)

Public telephone point

Automatic telephone exchange equipment

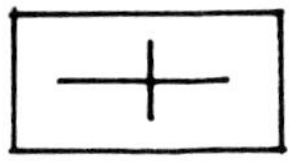

Automatic telex exchange equipment

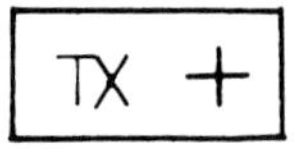

Manual switchboard

Fire protection

Hydrant point

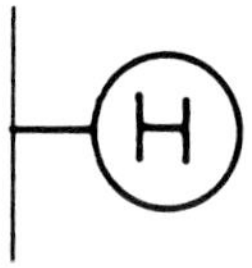

Wall valve—wet

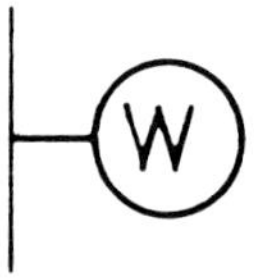

Wall valve—dry

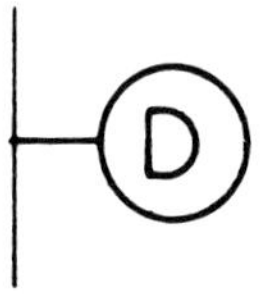

Hose reel

Fire extinguishers. Indicate type, e.g.
    SA Soda Acid
    W   Water
    F   Foam
    CO_2 Carbon dioxide etc.

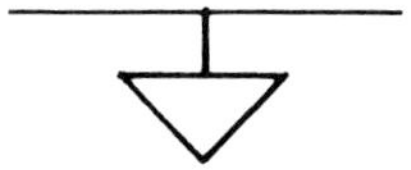

Sprinkler

Smoke detector

Heat detector

Alarm call point

Visual warning device

Audible warning device

Indicator panel

Appendix 5
Non-active lines and symbols

Co-ordinating dimension

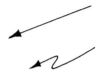

Modular dimension

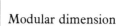

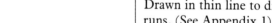

Other dimensions generally. The method, although recommended in most BSI literature, tends to be replaced in practice by the oblique slashes shown below
Most commonly used method for general dimensioning. Neat, legible and rapid

Leader lines, indicating where notes or descriptions apply

Centre lines or grid lines.
Drawn in thin line to distinguish them from service runs. (See Appendix 1)

Controlling line

Dotted line indicates important lines hidden in the particular plan or section view taken. (Also, on demolition drawings, work to be removed)

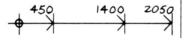

Running dimensions. Use should be restricted to surveys

Break line

Small dimensions are best indicated thus

Section line. The arrows point in the direction of view and the line joining them indicates the plane of the section

APPENDIX 5

✕ 27.305

Spot level—existing

✕ 27.305

Spot level—proposed

27.305
▽

Level shown on section or elevation—existing

27.305
▽

Level shown on section or elevation—proposed

Some abbreviations in common use

AD	above datum
app.	approximately
BM	bench mark
BSCP	British Standard Code of Practice
BSS	British Standard Specification
c/c	centre to centre
₵	centre line
diam.	diameter
dim.	dimension
exc.	excavate (excavation)
exg.	existing
Eq.	equal
extn.	extension
FFL	finished floor level
fin.	finish (finished)
FS	full size
fluor.	fluorescent
HD	heavy duty
HT	high tension
Htg.	heating
H/V (or H & V)	heating and ventilation
ID	internal diameter
inc.	including (inclusive)
int.	internal (interior)
IV	invert
LT	low tension
max.	maximum
mfr.	manufacturer
min.	minimum
misc.	miscellaneous
NBS	National Building Specification
nom.	nominal
NTS	not to scale
o/a	overall
OD	outside diameter
O/H	overhead
opp.	opposite
partn.	partition
PC	pre-cast
pr.	pair
prefab.	pre-fabricated
pt.	point (or part, depending on context)
rect.	rectangular (rectilinear)
reinf.	reinforced
rad.	radius
req.	required
ret.	return (returned)
sch.	schedule
spec.	specification
susp.	suspended
sq.	square
std.	standard
vert.	vertical
wt.	weight

Index to illustrations

Illustrations

1.1 Hellman's view of the problem 1
1.2 House at Gerrards Cross by A. Jessop Hardwick, c. 1905 2
1.3 Drawings, specification and bills of quantities 6
1.4 An early example of elementalisation 7
1.5 The fundamental search pattern generated by the questions Where?, What? and How? 8
1.6 Simple identification of components may be recorded on either a schedule or a location plan 9
1.7 The location plan is an inappropriate medium for recording the diverse characteristics of each component. Detail of this order can only be given elsewhere – in a specification or in other drawings to which the schedules point the way 9
1.8 The schedule provides a simple and economical index to a variety of information 9
1.9 The fundamental search pattern of **1.5** now runs through the schedule 10
1.10 The sub-component drawing illustrates how the component itself is made 10
1.11 Typical information drawing – this record of bore hole findings provides the contractor with useful background information but gives no instruction about the building 11
1.12 The complete primary structure of building drawings information 12
1.13 Drawing attempting to show everything ends up by showing nothing very clearly (scale 1:50). The information given on it, divided into its separate elements, is shown more legibly in the three following illustrations 13
1.14 Elemental version of **1.13** dealing with walls 14
1.15 Elemental version of **1.13** dealing with the floor 15
1.16 Elemental version of **1.13** dealing with doors 16
1.17 The fundamental search pattern 17
1.18 Search pattern running through different building elements 17
1.19 The simplest possible sub-division of building structure 18
1.20 Sub-division of building structure into structural elements 18
1.21 Further sub-division of the fabric leads to increasing complexity 18
2.1 Example of what can happen if site elements are not fully related. The manhole cover relates to neither the paving slabs nor the brick pavings 21
2.2 Site plan with inset assembly details is not to be recommended. Such details form no part of what is essentially a location drawing 22
2.3 A typical site plan. Information is given about new and existing levels and about paved surfaces, as well as directions as to where other information may be found 24
2.4 The basic plan. What to show and what not to (see the check list on p. 25) 26
2.5 Coded systems of finishes and over-elaborated written description on plans tend to be confusing 27
2.6 Finishes given in schedule form. Strong on descriptive detail though weak on actual location, it nevertheless offers a simple and effective method 28
2.7 Internal elevations on a room-by-room basis offer most flexible method for conveying information on finishes 28
2.8 Electrical layout at ceiling level 30
2.9 Air conditioning layout in ceiling void 30
2.10 Sprinkler layout at ceiling level 30
2.11 Architect's location drawing of the ceiling finishes provides co-ordinated layout for everyone involved 30
2.12 Floor plan or roof plan? The problem is avoided if all plans are treated as 'levels' 31
2.13 Elemental plan showing primary (2-) elements 33
2.14 Elemental plan showing secondary (3-) elements 34
2.15 Elemental plan showing (7-) fittings 35
2.16 Elementalisation used flexibly in practice. The (7–) location drawing shown gives a clear exposition of the responsibilities of one nominated sub-contractor – in this case the shopfitter 37
2.17 Elevation as location drawing 38
2.18 Location sections – designed to convey a general indication of what the contractor may expect rather than a detailed instruction of what he is to build 39
2.19 Elevation as a secondary reference to window components. The reference 'S(31) –' leads back to the

external wall secondary elements schedule where the components are listed and classified   41
2.20 Elevation as a guide to external finishes not easily indicated in detail by other means   42
2.21 Elevation as a schedule for pre-cast panels. Note the difference in method from that used in **2.19**. Here, with a limited range of panel types, and with each panel component drawing giving full information about it, the elevation itself forms an adequate schedule   43
2.22 Elevation giving information about external plumbing   44
2.23 Diagrammatic cross-section through a multi-storeyed building. Virtually all the information it gives may be conveyed more fully and intelligibly by other means – the frames will be built from the structural engineer's drawings; the doors will be manufactured from information to which the joiner is directed from the appropriate schedules, and will be installed in positions given on the floor plans; the construction of the external walls will be found on strip sections amplified as necessary by larger scale details. A cross-section such as that shown has its functions, but they are likely to be advisory – i.e. letting the contractor see the sort of building he is embarking upon – rather than directly instructing him what to build and where to build it   45
2.24 Sectional cut confined to perimeter of building   46
2.25 Location plan gives references to general sections L(--) and strip sections L(21). The former will be of the type shown in **2.23**. The latter will be similar in scope and function to that shown in **2.24**   47
2.26 How many window components in this assembly?   48
2.27 Six window components?   48
2.28 One window component?   48
2.29 The assembly is most sensibly regarded as having two window components, each being the largest single composite item within the supply of one manufacturer   48
2.30 Useful format for a door component drawing   49
2.31 External works components such as this lend themselves to standardisation. (Illustration from *Landscape Detailing* by Michael Littlewood, Architectural Press, London, 1984)   50
2.32 Shelving treated as a component rather than as an assembly. An example of common sense overriding too rigid theories of classification   50
2.33 Component detail of concrete cill   51
2.34 Component drawing of different doorsets all cross-referenced back to standard sub-component drawing (**2.35**)   52
2.35 Sub-component drawing illustrates constructional details of the component itself   53
2.36 Assembly detail from PSA Standard Library. Its simplicity contrasts sharply with the complexity of the detail illustrated in **2.37**. What they have in common is that each conveys clearly and precisely the information needed by the operative carrying out the assembly   54
2.37 Assembly detail from Willis Faber and Dumas Head Office Building (Foster Associates)   55
2.38 Not an easy task for any plasterer   56
2.39 Relatively simple detailing sensibly conveyed at a scale of 1:20   56
2.40 Scale of 1:5 is necessary to show this detailing adequately   57
2.41 Old-fashioned section through entire building. Far too detailed for its role of conveying information about the form and nature of the building; insufficient for anyone to build from with confidence   59
2.42 Location section provides references to where more detailed assembly information may be found   60
2.43 Assembly sections derived from **2.42**   61
2.44 Unnecessary elaboration wastes time and helps nobody   61
2.45 Simplified version of **2.44** gives adequate information to all concerned   61
2.46 Useful format for an openings schedule   62
2.47 'Vocabulary' type of schedule. It is dangerously easy to get a dot in the wrong place   63
2.48 Lists of ironmongery collected into sets   64
2.49 The openings schedule shown in **2.46** extended to give information about ironmongery sets   65
3.1 The range of line thicknesses available with the use of technical pens   68
3.2 Parts of three drawings using the Range 1 line thicknesses recommended in Table 1   69
3.3 The drawings shown in **3.2** re-drawn using the recommended Range 2 line thicknesses   70
3.4 Derivation of the rectangle A0 with a surface area of 1 square metre   71
3.5 'A' sizes retain the same proportions $(1:\sqrt{2})$. Each sheet is half the size of its predecessor   71
3.6 Overlapping smaller sheets allow the appropriate scale to be used for the plan of a large area without recourse to unwieldy A0 sheets   71
3.7 Key to sub-divided plan forms part of the title block   72
3.8 Various plastic cut-out templates available commercially   74
3.9 The co-ordinating dimension   75
3.10 The work size   75
3.11 Dimensional possibilities of window/wall assembly   75
3.12 Opening on plan defined by its co-ordinating dimension   76
3.13 Component destined to fill the opening shown in **3.12** is also defined by its co-ordinating dimension   76
3.14 Typical dimensioning of primary elements location plan   77
3.15 The controlling dimension   78
3.16 Vertical location of elements in the assembly section is given by reference to the planes established in **3.15**   78
3.17 Examples of different types of hand lettering   79
3.18 Formation of the upper case alphabet   80
3.19 A well-annotated plan (scale 1:20)   81
3.20 Commercially available lettering machine   82
3.21 Recommended method of folding 'A' size sheets always keeps the title panel visible   82
3.22 Example of drawing title panel   83
4.1 Final design drawing as issued to the client for approval   86
4.2 Copy negative taken from **4.1** before the blandishments were added   87
4.3 Print taken from **4.2** and marked up as a briefing guide to the drawing office at Stage E   88
4.4 Manufacturer's catalogue giving precise fixing details   89

4.5 Precedence diagram (taken from the RIBA *Management Handbook*) 90
4.6 A less sophisticated network, with the advantage that the time scale is immediately apparent 91
4.7 A print of the elevation has been used to identify every section through the external walls where the construction changes 93
4.8 A useful format for the drawing register. The explanatory notes help site staff as well as the drawing office 94
4.9 Status coding of a drawing indicates only its status at the present time 95
4.10 A full drawing number, using the system described 100
4.11 Drawings issue form accompanying *all* drawings provides a convenient file record of such issues 101
4.12 Histogram, taken from the records of an actual project, showing the difficulties of co-ordinating multi-disciplinary efforts 104
4.13 A drawing office programme allocates individual team members' appropriate work loads 105
5.1 Demolition drawing covering formation of new opening in an existing wall 107
5.2 Drawing covering installation of new door and frame in the opening formed in **5.1** 107
5.3 Demolition drawing of reflected ceiling plan 108
5.4 Drawing showing new works replacing demolitions shown in **5.3** 109
5.5 Basic location plan is shown here in the overlay drafting method separated into four constituent negatives 110
5.6 and **5.7** Negatives from other consultants are added as overlays to selected negatives from the architect's original basic drawings to produce composite interprints 111
5.8 Complexities of photographic and printing sequences demand proper administrative control 112
5.9 Modular discipline eliminates the need for complicated dimensioning by limiting the location of elements to certain standard situations 112
5.10 Part of a working drawing produced by a digital plotter for DHSS Harness hospitals project 113
5.11 Computer not only shows assembly in perspective but has the ability to change the view-point at will 114
5.12 Plan view of **5.11** 115
5.13 A typical high resolution graphics work station 115
5.14 DHSS computer application in total Health Buildings system 116

Index

Illustrations are listed separately

assembly drawing 7, 30, 52, 55, 59, 95
    standard details in 89–90
axonometric drawings, use of 64
bills of quantities 4, 10, 17, 110
building construction 3, 5, 36, 55
building contractor 3, 72, 101–2, 110
building element
    examples 118–9
    references to in drawings 40, 72
    structuring drawings by 17, 19, 25, 32
building materials 3, 122–3
Building Research Establishment 2, 76
CI/SfB system 18–20, 25, 30, 32, 40, 55, 62, 85, 92, 95, 103, 105, 107
coding 59, 95, 103
common arrangement 117
component drawing 7, 40, 46, 49, 52, 95
    standard details in 90–1
    standard format for 49
computer graphics 113–6
conventions 72–3, 120–1
conversion, alteration and rehabilitation, drawing methods for 106–7
Co-ordinating Committee for Project Information 4
data sheets 85
design, drawings to show 84–5
demolition 106
design team, programme of work for 91, 103, 104–5
detail paper 66
diazo copying 66
dimensioning 74–8, 112–3
distribution of drawings 100–1
drafting film 67, 110, 111
drawing materials 66–7
drawing register 95
    maintenance and circulation 100
drawing techniques 67–8, 73, 74, 110, 112–3
dyeline copying *see* diazo copying
electro-static copying 66
elevations
    as part of location plans 92
    details needed for various purposes 40
    schematic 36

elevation sheet
    internal 25
extensions 106
floor plan 23, 25
format 49, 103
grids 112–3
Guide on Resource Control see RIBA
Handbook of Architectural Practice and Management 2
hatching 73
information drawing 10
ink as drawing material 67
lettering
    by hand 79–80
    by stencil 80
    by transfer 80
    by typewriter or machine 80
    using film 80
liaison with other professionals 102–3
line thickness 25, 67–8
location drawing 7, 10, 21, 23, 30, 32, 36–40, 92, 103
    as operational bill of quantities 110
    coding of in packages 59
    elevation 36
    sections 40, 95
National Building Specification 85
office management *see* design team
office manual as drawings guide 101–2
operational bill of quantities *see* bills of quantities
overlay draughting 110
paper
    size 36, 66, 68, 71–2
    type 66–7
pencil
    as drawing material 67
    techniques 68
pen, types of for various purposes 67–8
pictorial drawings 64
perspective drawings, use of 64
photomontage, use of 64
plan of work 84
production drawings 103, 104, 111
programme of work *see* design team
RIBA
    Plan of Work 84
    Management Handbook (*Guide on Resource Control*) 91

reproduction
    materials for 66–7
    processes used in 66
    techniques in drawing for 67
scale 32, 36, 55, 57, 72, 92, 112
schedule 7–8, 10, 32, 95
    types of 59, 62
    see also data sheets
section drawings
    as part of location plans 92, 95
site plan
    as part of location drawing 92
    functions of 21–3
source document for specification and working drawings 85
specification 4, 17, 64, 85
standard details 89–90
statutory approval 84
storage of drawings 100, 103
structural engineer, responsibility of 32
    see also liaison with other professionals
'Structuring Project Information' 12, 106
sub-component drawing 10, 52, 72
symbols
    electrical 73
    examples 122–9
    stick-on and dry transfer 74
    templates for 73–4
title panel 80, 82
tracing paper 66–7
trade literature, use of 89
working drawings
    code of practice for 4
    details 55, 59, 85
    draft 85
    guide to 101–2
    management 84–105
    position of title panel 80
    plan of work for 3
    problems in 2, 12, 23, 55
    scale 32, 55, 103
    structure of 4–5, 6, 17, 104–5
    user's needs from 3, 5, 7, 103
    see also assembly drawings; component drawings; location drawings

The bestselling quartet
MANUAL OF GRAPHIC TECHNIQUES 1-4

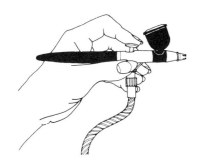 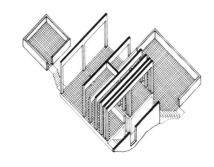 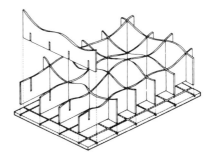 

Volume 1

Tom Porter and Bob Greenstreet

Surface, line and tone
Colour: mediums and methods
Orthographics and perspective drawings
Reprographic and simulation techniques
Presentation and exhibition

1980   128pp   over 400 illus   210 × 297 mm
paper   ISBN 0 906525 17 9

Volume 2

Tom Porter and Sue Goodman

Anatomy of an image
Mechanics of representation
Basic mark-making techniques
Graphics without tears
The presentation package

1982   128pp   over 500 illus   210 × 297 mm
paper   ISBN 0 906525 24 1

Volume 3

Tom Porter and Sue Goodman

Lettering design
Drawing and design for reproduction
Basic printmaking processes
Modelmaking techniques

1983   128pp   over 400 illus   210 × 297 mm
paper   ISBN 0 906525 25 X

Volume 4

Tom Porter and Sue Goodman

Plans
Elevations
Sections
Axonometrics and isometrics
Perspectives

1985   128pp   over 400 illus   210 × 297 mm
paper   ISBN 0 906525 26 8

'The techniques are well taught and the step-by-step instructions are clear... I shall be recommending the manual to my students.' **Robert Lee, Designers' Journal**

Price £8.95 each volume (N.B. Prices are subject to change without notice)

Astragal Books
An imprint of
The Architectural Press
9 Queen Anne's Gate
London SW1H 9BY

ARCHITECTURAL PRESS
AP

Two Classic Drawing Books

Measured Drawing for Architects

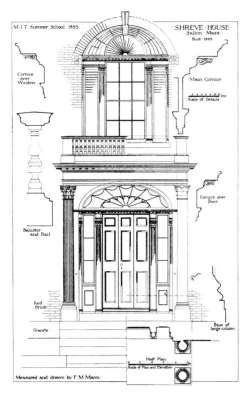

Robert Chitham

'This eminently readable and practical manual gives both a history of measured drawing and an examination of the business of on-site surveying, measuring and estimating dimensions and the production of finished drawings.'
Building Design

'Mr Chitham writes with a wit and humanity most uncommon in technical books...strongly recommended.' **Society of Architectural Historians of Great Britain Newsletter**

Contents:
Introduction
The purpose of measured drawing.
Historical review.
Measuring on the site.
Drawing up surveys.
Plates.

*1980   128pp   82 b/w illus   297 × 210 mm
paper   ISBN 0 85139 392 6   £10.95**

The Classical Orders of Architecture

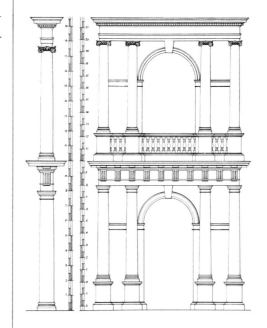

Robert Chitham

'Long overdue...a useful primer for students to grasp the proportions and profiles of the orders, before moving on to the older and heavier works of the masters.' **Quinlan Terry**

'Excellent...I hope many architects and students buy it...and make good use of it.'
Robert Adam, The Architects' Journal

Contents:
Introduction
Historical background.
The orders in detail.
Use of the orders.
Glossary.
Bibliography.

50 pages of original line drawings.
*1985   160pp   297 × 210 mm   paper
ISBN 0 85139 779 4   £14.95**

*Prices are subject to change without notice.

**The Architectural Press
9 Queen Anne's Gate
London SW1H 9BY**

ARCHITECTURAL PRESS